THE
LITTLE GIANT®
ENCYCLOPEDIA
OF

Inspirational
Quotes

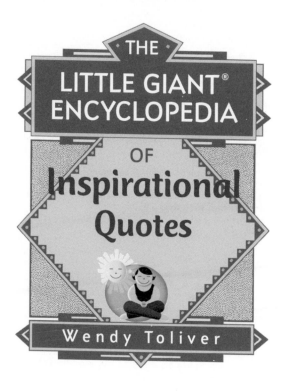

THE
LITTLE GIANT® ENCYCLOPEDIA

OF
Inspirational Quotes

Wendy Toliver

Sterling Publishing Co., Inc.
New York

Compiled by: Wendy Toliver
Book Design: Jennifer Luman

The author has strived to be as accurate as possible with the exact wording of direct quotes and with the attribution to original sources listed in the book. Our apology in advance for the misrepresentation or inaccuracy due to the reprinting of sources.

Library of Congress Cataloging-in-Publication Data

Toliver, Wendy.
 The little giant encyclopedia of inspirational quotes / compiled by
 Wendy Toliver
    p. cm.
 Includes bibliographical references and index.
 ISBN 1-4027-1159-X
 1. Conduct of life—Quotations, maxims, etc. 2. Inspirational—
Quotations, maxims, etc. I. Toliver, Wendy.
PN6084. C556L58 2004
082—dc22

2004003131

10 9 8 7 6 5 4 3 2 1
Published by Sterling Publishing Co., Inc.
387 Park Avenue South, New York, NY 10016
© 2004 by Wendy Toliver
Distributed in Canada by Sterling Publishing
c/o Manda Group, 165 Dufferin Street
Toronto, Ontario, Canada M6K 3H6
Distributed in Great Britain by Chrysalis Books Group PLC,
The Chrysalis Building, Bramley Road, London W10 6SP, England
Distributed in Australia by Capricorn Link (Australia) Pty. Ltd.
P. O. Box 704, Windsor, NSW 2756, Australia
Printed and Bound in China
All Rights Reserved

Sterling ISBN 1-4027-1159-X

Contents

Advice 11
Aging Gracefully and Maturity 15
Art 31
Beauty 43
Bravery 49
Change, Progress & Growth 57
Character & Personality 71
Children & Youth 87
Criticism 99
Determination 105
Education 107
Effort & Labor 123
Equality 131
Experience 137
Faith 141
Fate & Destiny 145
Freedom 147
Friendship 155
Fun & Play 165
The Future 169
Genius 173
Giving, Service & Charity 177
Goals & Direction 185
God & Angels 193
Greatness 203
Happiness 209

Heroism 219
Hopes & Dreams 223
Humbleness 231
Imagination 235
Journey 239
Justice 247
Kindness 251
Laughter & Smiles 255
Liberty 261
Life 267
Limitless Possibilities 279
Love 283
Nature 295
Optimism 307
Parenthood 315
Patience 323
Patriotism 327
Peace & Nonviolence 333
Perseverance & Persistence 339
Preparation 349
Reason 351
Relationships 353
Rewards 361
Self-Esteem & Confidence 365
Silence & Brevity 373
Simple Pleasures 381
Success 387
Taking Action 399

Taking Chances & Taking Risks 409
Taking Charge & Taking Control 417
Time 419
Trust 429
Truth 433
Uniqueness 445
Virtues 447
Wealth 453
Wisdom & Knowledge 461
The World 475
Bibliography 479
Index 485

Introduction

Many things in the world inspire us. People such as parents, teachers, coaches, social and religious leaders, and others we respect—whether an acquaintance or a historical figure we've studied—help us grow and improve our lives. The world around us, the spirituality deep within us, and our experiences during our lifetime all help us realize our limitless possibilities.

In collecting quotations and writings for this book, I sorted through a vast variety of sources and compiled a truly thought-provoking collection of inspirational tidbits. Some are emotional, some philosophical, some humorous, and some a bit off-the-wall.

The book is divided into categorical chapters, which are presented in alphabetical order. Because each quotation means something different to each reader, I categorized each quotation as I guessed most people would categorize it. If you like a certain person's opinion or thought process based on an excerpt here in, I challenge you to research that person, read some of his or her works, watch his or her movies, study his or her art, listen to his or her music, or possibly even talk to him or her. Putting this book together has been a wonderful journey, and I thank all the people who contributed their thoughts and opinions to help inspire all of us.

By necessity, by proclivity, and
by delight, we all quote.
—*Ralph Waldo Emerson*

I quote others only to better express myself.
—*Michel E. de Montaigne*

How do people go to sleep? I'm afraid I've lost
the knack . . . I might repeat to myself, slowly and sooth-
ingly, a list of quotations beautiful from minds
profound; if I can remember any of the damn things.
—*Dorothy Parker*

I often quote myself; it adds spice to my conversation.
—*George Bernard Shaw*

I didn't really say everything I said.
—*Yogi Berra*

The wisdom of the wise, and the experience
of ages, may be preserved by quotation.
—*Benjamin Disraeli*

Advice

All of us, at certain moments of our lives, need to take
advice and to receive help from other people.
—*Alexis Carrel*

Keep breathing.
—*Sophie Tucker*

This is what you shall do: Love the earth and sun
and the animals, despise riches, give alms to every
one that asks, stand up for the stupid and crazy,
devote your income and labor to others, hate
tyrants, argue not concerning God.
—*Walt Whitman*

Eutrapelia. "A happy and gracious flexibility," Pericles
calls this quality of the Athenians . . . lucidity of
thought, cleanness and propriety of language, freedom
from prejudice and freedom from stiffness, openness
of mind, amiability of manners.
—*Matthew Arnold*

Desire, ask, believe, receive.
—*Stella Terrill Mann*

Keep your head up, keep your shoulders back,
keep your self-respect, be nice, be smart.
—*Lucille Ball*

Be on the alert, stand firm in the faith,
act like men, be strong.
—*adapted from 1 Corinthians 16:13*

Moderation in all things.
—*Terence*

The greatest thing in the world is
to know how to belong to oneself.
—*Michel E. de Montaigne*

Law is order, and good law is good order.
—*Aristotle*

I leave this rule for others when I'm dead,
Enrich yourselves!

—*François Guizot*

———————

Surely the shortest commencement address in history—
and for me one of the most memorable—was that of Dr.
Harold E. Hyde, President of New Hampshire's Plymouth
State College. He reduced his message to the graduating
class to these three ideals: "Know yourself—Socrates.
Control yourself—Cicero. Give yourself—Christ."

—*Walter T. Tatara*

———————

Always look out for Number One and
be careful not to step in Number Two.

—*Rodney Dangerfield*

———————

Speak in French when you can't think of the
English for a thing—turn out your toes when you
walk—and remember who you are!

—*Lewis Carroll*

Man was made for joy and woe,
And when this we rightly know
Through the world we safely go.
—*William Blake*

He who is of a calm and happy nature will hardly feel
the pressure of age, but to him who is of an opposite
disposition young and age are equally a burden.
—*Plato*

Instead of dirt and poison we have rather chosen
to fill our hives with honey and wax; thus
furnishing mankind with the two noblest
of things, which are sweetness and light.
—*Jonathan Swift*

Aging Gracefully & Maturity

To know how to grow old is the masterwork of wisdom, and
one of the most difficult chapters in the great art of living.
—*Henri Frédéric Amiel*

If wrinkles must be written upon our brows,
let them not be written upon the heart.
The spirit should never grow old.
—*James A. Garfield*

The secret of staying young is to live honestly,
eat slowly, and lie about your age.
—*Lucille Ball*

It is the height of absurdity to sow little but weeds
in the first half of one's lifetime and expect to harvest
a valuable crop in the second half.
—*Percy Johnston*

I believe that the sign of maturity is
accepting deferred gratification.
—*Peggy Cahn*

You ought not to practice childish ways,
since you are no longer that age.

—*Homer*

A beautiful lady is an accident of nature.
A beautiful old lady is a work of art.

—*Louis Nizer*

Wrinkles should merely indicate
where the smiles have been.

—*Mark Twain*

How old would you be if
you didn't know how old you were?

—*Satchel Paige*

Cherish all your happy moments: they
make a fine cushion for old age.

—*Booth Tarkington*

To live with grace we must be prepared to die with grace.

—*Arnold Beisser*

I prefer old age to the alternative.
—*Maurice Chevalier*

I believe that the sign of maturity is
accepting deferred gratification.
—*Peggy Cahn*

And as for you, you shall go to your fathers in peace;
you shall be buried at a good old age.
—*adapted from Genesis 15:15*

Age . . . is a matter of feeling, not of years.
—*George William Curtis*

To grow mature is to separate more
distinctly, to connect more closely.
—*Hugo von Hofmannsthal*

Our message: Don't grow up. Growing up
means giving up your dreams.
—*Jerry Rubin*

The mark of the immature man is that he wants
to die nobly for a cause, while the mark of a mature
man is that he wants to live humbly for one.

—*Wilhelm Stekel*

The whole business of marshaling one's energies becomes
more and more important as one grows older.

—*Hume Cronyn*

Age does not depend upon years, but
upon temperament and health. Some men
are born old, and some never grow so.

—*Tryon Edwards*

I find that a man is as old as his work. If his
work keeps him from moving forward, he will
look forward with the work.

—*William Ernest Hocking*

The more sand that has escaped from the hourglass of
our life, the clearer we should see through it.

—*Jean Paul*

A man is not old as long as he is seeking something.
—*Jean Rostand*

I'm supposed to be old. But I feel great, like a kid.
—*Cher*

Though it sounds absurd, it is true to say I
felt younger at sixty than I felt at twenty.
—*Ellen Glasgow*

Older men are to be temperate, dignified, sensible, sound
in faith, in love, in perseverance. Older women likewise
are to be reverent in their behavior, not malicious gossips,
nor enslaved to much wine, teaching what is good.
—*adapted from Titus 2:2–3*

Fifty—the age of youth, the youth of old age.
—*William Powell*

Therefore I summon age
To grant youth's heritage.
—*Robert Browning*

In your 20s, you feel like you're indestructible, that nothing can kill you and you laugh at death. You go on and stay up for days and do as many things as you can and then, in your 30s, you think, well, maybe I'll be around here a little longer, so I'm going to maybe take better care of myself.

—*John Belushi*

I suppose everyone continues to be interested in the quest for the self, but what you feel when you're older, I think is that . . . you really must make the self. It is absolutely useless to look for it, you won't find it, but it's possible in some sense to make it. I don't mean in the sense of making a mask, a Yeatsian mask. But you finally begin in some sense to make and choose the self you want.

—*Mary McCarthy*

To me, old age is always fifteen years older than I am.

—*Bernard Baruch*

You don't stop laughing because you grow old; you grow old because you stop laughing.

—*Michael Pritchard*

The older woman's love is not love of herself, nor of herself mirrored in a lover's eyes, nor is it corrupted by need. It is a feeling of tenderness so still and deep and warm that it gilds every grassblade and blesses every fly. It includes the ones who have a claim on it, and a great deal else besides. I wouldn't have missed it for the world.

—*Germaine Greer*

Old age is not a disease—it is strength and survivorship, triumph over all kinds of vicissitudes and disappointments, trials and illnesses.

—*Maggie Kuhn*

If you associate enough with older people who do enjoy their lives . . . you will gain a sense of continuity and of the possibility for a full life.

—*Margaret Mead*

As a white candle
In a holy place
So is the beauty
Of an aged face.

—*Joseph Campbell*

The young man knows the rules but
the old man knows the exceptions.
—*Oliver Wendell Holmes*

I speak the truth, not so much as I would, but as much
as I dare; and I dare a little more, as I grow older.
—*Michel E. de Montaigne*

The belief that youth is the happiest time of life is
founded upon a fallacy. The happiest person is the
person who thinks the most interesting thoughts,
and we grow happier as we grow older.
—*William Lyon Phelps*

I do beseech you to direct your efforts more
to preparing youth for the path and less to
preparing the path for the youth.
—*Ben Lindsey*

Whom the gods love, die young,
no matter how long they live.
—*Elbert Hubbard*

The interests of childhood and youth
are the interest of mankind.
—*Edmund Storer James*

Don't laugh at a youth for his affections; he's only
trying on one face after another till he finds his own.
—*Logan Pearsall Smith*

The Youth of a Nation are the trustees of posterity.
—*Benjamin Disraeli*

My poetry doesn't change from place to place—
it changes with the years. It's very important to be
one's age. You get ideas you have to turn down—
"I'm sorry, no longer": "I'm sorry, not yet."
—*W. H. Auden*

Real maturity is the ability to imagine the humanity of
every person as fully as you believe in your own humanity.
—*Tobias Wolff*

To know how to grow old is the masterwork
of wisdom, and one of the most difficult
chapters in the great art of living.
—*Henri Frédéric Amiel*

Take kindly the counsel of the years, gracefully
surrendering the things of youth.
—*Max Ehrmann*

Growing up is after all only the understanding that one's
unique and incredible experience is what everyone shares.
—*Doris Lessing*

Happy the man who gains sagacity in youth, but thrice
happy he who retains the fervour of youth in age.
—*Dagobert Runes*

Anyone who stops learning is old, whether at twenty
or eighty. Anyone who keeps learning stays young. The
greatest thing in life is to keep your mind young.
—*Henry Ford*

How beautifully the leaves grow old. How
full of light and colour are their last days.
—*John Burroughs*

A mark of maturity seems to be the range and extent
of one's feeling or self-involvement in abstract ideas.
—*Gordon Allport*

The closing years of life are like the end of a masquerade
party, when the masks are dropped.
—*Arthur Schopenhauer*

The mark of a mature man is the ability to give
love and receive it joyously and without guilt.
—*Leo Baeck*

Maturity is the capacity to endure uncertainty.
—*John Finley*

It is not white hair that endangers wisdom.
—*Menander*

No wise man ever wished to be younger.
—*Jonathan Swift*

Grow up, and that is a terribly hard thing to do. It is much easier to skip it and go from one childhood to another.
—*F. Scott Fitzgerald*

We grow neither better nor worse as we get old, but more like ourselves.
—*Mary Lamberton Becker*

To keep the heart unwrinkled, to be hopeful, kindly, cheerful, reverent—that is to triumph over old age.
—*Thomas Bailey Aldrich*

The immature mind hops from one thing to another; the mature mind seeks to follow through.
—*Harry A. Overstreet*

We do not count a man's years until he has nothing else to count.
—*Ralph Waldo Emerson*

How pleasant it is that always there's
somebody older than you.

—*Florence Smith*

You are never too young to fall in love
and never too old to wish you had.

—*Carrie Noble*

Happy old man!

—*Virgil*

Old men are children for a second time.

—*Aristophanes*

Nature gives you the face you have at twenty;
it is up to you to merit the face you have at fifty.

—*Coco Chanel*

We don't stop playing because we grow old,
we grow old because we stop playing.

—*George Bernard Shaw*

To be seventy years young is sometimes far more
cheerful and hopeful than to be forty years old.
—*Elbert Hubbard*

Old indeed! There's many a
good tune played on an old fiddle!
—*Samuel Butler*

What through youth gave love and roses,
Age still gives us friends and wine.
—*Thomas Moore*

They say an old man is twice a child.
—*William Shakespeare*

Young men think old men are fools; but old
men know young men are fools.
—*George Chapman*

But though an old man, I am but a young gardener.
—*Thomas Jefferson*

People are unreasonable, illogical and self-centered.
Love them anyway.
If you do good, people will accuse you of selfish, ulterior motives.
Do good anyway.
If you are successful, you will win false friends and true enemies.
Succeed anyway.
The good you do today will be forgotten tomorrow.
Do good anyway.
Honesty and frankness make you vulnerable.
Be honest and frank anyway.
The biggest person with the biggest ideas can be shot down
by the smallest person with the smallest mind.
Think big anyway.
What you spend years building may be destroyed overnight.
Build anyway.
People really need help but may attack if you help them.
Help people anyway.
Wherever there is a human being, there is an opportunity for kindness.
—*Lucius Annaeus Seneca*

Maturity consists of no longer being taken in by oneself.
—*Kajetan von Schlaggenberg*

The longer I live the more beautiful life becomes.
—*Frank Lloyd Wright*

Age cannot wither her, no custom stale
Her infinite variety.
—*William Shakespeare*

The cheerful live longest in years, and afterwards in our regards. Cheerfulness is the offshoot of goodness.
—*Christian Nestell Bovee*

Art

Life without industry is guilt,
industry without art is brutality.
—*John Ruskin*

———

Art is the signature of civilization.
—*Beverly Sills*

———

Art teaches nothing, except the significance of life.
—*Henry Miller*

———

Art is much less important than life,
but what a poor life without it!
—*Robert Motherwell*

———

Art must unquestionably have a social value; that is,
as a potential means of communication it must
be addressed, and in comprehensible terms,
to the understanding of mankind.
—*Rockwell Kent*

All that I desire to point out is the general principle
that Life imitates Art far more than Art imitates Life.

—*Oscar Wilde*

An artist cannot fail; it is a success to be one.

—*Charles Horton Cooley*

The defining function of the
artist is to cherish consciousness.

—*Max Eastman*

Art is a collaboration between God and the artist,
and the less the artist does the better.

—*André Gide*

If art is to nourish the roots of our culture, society must set
the artist free to follow his vision wherever it takes him.

—*John F. Kennedy*

Art hath an enemy called Ignorance.

—*Ben Jonson*

I saw the angel in the marble
and carved until I set him free.

—*Michelangelo*

———•———

I feel there are territories within us that are totally
unknown. Huge, mysterious, and dangerous territories.
We think we know ourselves, when we really know
only this little bitty part. We have this social persona
that we present to each other. We have all these galaxies
inside of us. And if we don't enter those in art of one
kind or another, whether it's playwriting, or paint,
or music, or whatever, then I don't understand the
point of doing anything. It's the reason I write. I
try to go into parts of myself that are unknown.

—*Sam Shepard*

———•———

Art is a fruit that grows in man, like a fruit
on a plant, or a child in its mother's womb.

—*Jean Arp*

———•———

Art attracts us only by what it
reveals of our most secret self.

—*Jean-Luc Godard*

Art is an effort to create, beside the
real world, a more human world.
—*André Maurois*

Great art is as irrational as great music.
It is mad with its own loveliness.
—*George Jean Nathan*

Art for art's sake? I should think so, and more so than
ever at the present time. It is the one orderly product
which our middling race has produced. It is the cry of
a thousand sentinels, the echo from a thousand labyrinths,
it is the lighthouse which cannot be hidden . . . it is the
best evidence we have of our dignity.
—*E. M. Forster*

Art is the most intense mode of
individualism that the world has known.
—*Oscar Wilde*

Art is an experience, not the formulation of a problem.
—*Lindsay Anderson*

God is really only another artist. He invented the giraffe, the elephant, and the cat. He has no real style. He just keeps on trying new things.

—*Pablo Picasso*

All art requires courage.

—*Anne Tucker*

One thing that makes art different from life is that in art things have a shape . . . it allows us to fix our emotions on events that the moment they occur, it permits a union of heart and mind and tongue and tear.

—*Marilyn French*

The arts are an even better barometer of what is happening in our world than the stock market or the debates in congress.

—*Hendrik Willem van Loon*

I am for an art that imitates the human, that is comic, if necessary, or violent, or whatever is necessary.

—*Claes Oldenburg*

Art is not a treasure in the past or an importation
from another land, but part of the present life
of all the living and creating peoples.
—*Franklin D. Roosevelt*

Vision is the art of seeing things invisible.
—*Jonathan Swift*

Un croquis vaut mieux qu'un long discours.
(A picture is worth a thousand words.)
—*Napoleon Bonaparte*

Art is the objectification of feeling.
—*Susanne K. Langer*

A work of art is above all an adventure of the mind.
—*Eugène Ionesco*

Great art is an instant arrested in eternity.
—*James G. Huneker*

Art is the reason for living, today as in the past.
—*Hans-Jurgen Syberberg*

Art is so wonderfully irrational, exuberantly
pointless, but necessary, all the same.
—*Günter Grass*

No great artist ever sees things as they really are.
If he did, he would cease to be an artist.
—*Oscar Wilde*

Art is a human activity having for its purpose the
transmission to others of the highest and best
feelings to which men have risen.
—*Leo Tolstoy*

Still, there is a calm, pure harmony, and music inside of me.
—*Vincent van Gogh*

The scholar seeks, the artist finds.
—*André Gide*

Art is the soul of a people.
—*Romare Bearden*

The truest expression of a people
is in its dances and its music.
—*Agnes de Mille*

Supreme art is a traditional statement of certain heroic
and religious truth, passed on from age to age, modified
by individual genius, but never abandoned.
—*William Butler Yeats*

Art is the stored honey of the human soul,
gathered on wings of misery and travail.
—*Theodore Dreiser*

Art is a human activity, consisting in this, that one
man consciously, by means of external signs, hands on
to others feelings he has worked through, and other people
are infected by these feelings and also experience them.
—*Leo Tolstoy*

The true work of art is but
a shadow of the divine perfection.
—*Michelangelo*

I cry out for order and find it only in art.
—*Helen Hayes*

Art is a staple of mankind—never a by-product
of elitism. So urgent, so utterly linked with the pulse
of feeling that it becomes the singular sign of life when
every other aspect of civilization fails. . . . Like hunger
and sex, it is a disposition of the human cell—a marvelous
fiction of the brain which recreates itself as something
as mysterious as mind. Art is consistent with every
aspect of every day in the life of every people.
—*Jamake Highwater*

Art is not a thing: it is a way.
—*Elbert Hubbard*

True art is eternal, but it is not stationary.
—*Otto H. Kahn*

Art is the window to man's soul. Without it, he would never be able to see beyond his immediate world; nor could the world see the man within.
—*Claudia (Lady Bird) Johnson*

When power leads man toward arrogance, poetry reminds him of his limitations. When power narrows the areas of man's concern, poetry reminds him of the richness and diversity of his experience. When power corrupts, poetry cleanses. For art establishes the basic human truths which must serve as the touchstones of our judgement. The artist . . . faithful to his personal vision of reality, becomes the last champion of the individual mind and sensibility against an intrusive society and an offensive state.
—*John F. Kennedy*

Art is the most passionate orgy within man's grasp.
—*Jean Dubuffet*

If you ask me what I came to do in this world, I, an artist, I will answer you: "I am here to live out loud."
—*Emile Zola*

Art washes away from the soul the dust of everyday life.
—*Pablo Picasso*

It is not in life but in art that
self-fulfillment is to be found.
—*George Woodcock*

Art is man's nature: nature is God's art.
—*P. J. Bailey*

We must never forget that art is not a form
of propaganda; it is a form of truth.
—*John F. Kennedy*

The art of a people is a true mirror of their minds.
—*Jawaharlal Nehru*

Art is good when it springs from necessity. This kind
of origin is the guarantee of its value; there is no other.
—*Neal Cassady*

Every artist dips his brush into his own soul,
and paints his own nature into his pictures.
—*Henry Ward Beecher*

Art is the desire of a man to express himself, to record
the reactions of his personality to the world he lives in.
—*Amy Lowell*

Art is not an end in itself, but
a means of addressing humanity.
—*Modest Mussorgsky*

We look too much to museums. The sun
coming up in the morning is enough.
—*Ralph Ellison*

To speak of morals in art is to speak of legislature
in sex. Art is the sex of the imagination.
—*George Jean Nathan*

Beauty

All beauty comes from beautiful blood
and a beautiful brain.

—*Walt Whitman*

One of the few advantages to not being beautiful
is that one usually gets better-looking as one gets older;
I am, in fact, at this very moment gaining my looks.

—*Nora Ephron*

Though we travel the world over to find the
beautiful, we must carry it with us or we find it not.

—*Ralph Waldo Emerson*

Our hearts were drunk with beauty
Our eyes could never see.

—*George W. Russell*

Warm, dark and handsome.

—*Mae West*

Better an ugly face than an ugly mind.
—*James Ellis*

The beautiful people.
—*Diana Vreeland*

People who are very beautiful make their own laws.
—*Vivien Leigh*

Beauty is altogether in the eye of the beholder.
—*Lew Wallace*

Beauty is not caused. It is.
—*Emily Dickinson*

Character contributes to beauty. It fortifies a woman
as her youth fades. A mode of conduct, a standard
of courage, discipline, fortitude and integrity can do
a great deal to make a woman beautiful.
—*Jacqueline Bisset*

There is no cosmetic for beauty like happiness.
—*Lady Blessington*

Hallow the body as a temple to comeliness and sanctify the heart as a sacrifice to love; love recompenses the adorers.
—*Kahlil Gibran*

Beauty is one of the rare things that
do not lead to doubt of God.
—*Jean Anouilh*

Beauty is power; a smile is a sword.
—*Charles Reade*

Beauty like hers is genius.
—*Dante Gabriel Rossetti*

Beauty without grace is the hook without the bait.
—*Ralph Waldo Emerson*

Truth exists for the wise, beauty for the feeling heart.
—*Johann von Schiller*

Beauty in all things—no, we cannot
hope for that; but some place set apart for it.
—*Edna St. Vincent Millay*

[I]t is the spirit that knows Beauty, that has music in its
soul and the color of sunsets in its headkerchiefs; that can
dance on a flaming world and make the world dance, too.
—*W. E. B. Du Bois*

If beauty isn't genius it usually signals
at least a high level of animal cunning.
—*Peter York*

Mind, mind alone, bear witness, earth and heaven!
The living fountains in itself contains
Of beauteous and sublime.
—*Mark Akenside*

Beauty is truth—truth, beauty—that is all Ye
know on earth, and all ye need to know.
—*John Keats*

In every man's heart there is a secret nerve
that answers to the vibrations of beauty.
—*Christopher Morley*

Beauty is all that counts, pal. That's all that counts.
—*Jack Nicholson*

Beauty is only skin deep, but it's a valuable
asset if you're poor or haven't any sense.
—*Kin Hubbard*

Beauty is an ecstasy; it is as simple as hunger.
There is really nothing to be said about it.
—*W. Somerset Maugham*

Beauty is the gift of God.
—*Aristotle*

Things are beautiful if you love them.
—*Jean Anouilh*

———•———

Beauty in things exists in the mind
which contemplates them.
—*David Hume*

———•———

The definition of a beautiful woman is one who loves me.
—*Sloan Wilson*

———•———

A thing of beauty is a joy forever:
Its loveliness increases; it will never
Pass into nothingness; but still will keep
A bower quiet for us, and a sleep
Full of sweet dreams, and health, and quiet breathing.
—*John Keats*

———•———

The best and most beautiful things in the world
cannot be seen or even touched—they must
be felt with the heart.
—*Helen Keller*

Bravery

No coward soul is mine,
No trembler in the world's storm-troubled sphere:
I see Heaven's glories shine,
And faith shines equal, arming me from fear.
—*Emily Brontë*

Courage is fear holding on a minute longer.
—*George S. Patton*

The greatest test of courage on earth
is to bear defeat without losing heart.
—*Robert Green Ingersoll*

A timid person is frightened before a danger, a coward
during the time, and a courageous person afterwards.
—*Jean Paul Richter*

It takes vision and courage to create—
it takes faith and courage to prove.
—*Owen D. Young*

The surest way to prevent war is not to fear it.
—*John Randolph*

We confide in our strength, without boasting of it; we respect that of others, without fearing it.
—*Thomas Jefferson*

What would you do if you knew you could not fail?
—*Robert Schuller*

What would life be if we had
no courage to attempt anything?
—*Vincent van Gogh*

Valour lies just halfway between rashness and cowardice.
—*Miguel de Cervantes*

Don't be afraid to take a big step if one is indicated. You can't cross a chasm in two small jumps.
—*David Lloyd George*

The guts carry the feet, not the feet the guts.
—*Miguel de Cervantes*

Courage—fear that has said its prayers.
—*Dorothy Bernard*

Far better it is to dare mighty things, to win glorious triumphs, even though checkered by failure, than to take rank with those poor spirits who neither enjoy much nor suffer much, because they live in the grey twilight that knows not victory nor defeat.
—*Theodore Roosevelt*

Bravery is the capacity to perform properly even when scared half to death.
—*Omar Bradley*

Courage is rightly esteemed the first of human qualities because it is the quality which guarantees all others.
—*Winston Churchill*

This is no time for ease and comfort.
It is the time to dare and endure.
—*Winston Churchill*

The wicked flee when no one is pursuing,
but the righteous are as bold as a lion.
—*adapted from Proverbs 28:1*

Courage takes many forms. There is physical
courage, there is moral courage. Then there is a still
higher type of courage—the courage to brave pain,
to live with it, to never let others know of it and
to still find joy in life; to wake up in the morning
with an enthusiasm for the day ahead.
—*Howard Cosell*

This will remain the land of the free only
so long as it is the home of the brave.
—*Elmer Davis*

Brave men are brave from the very first.
—*Pierre Corneille*

One man with courage makes a majority.
—*Andrew Jackson*

Life shrinks or expands in proportion to one's courage.
—*Anaïs Nin*

Who bravely dares must sometimes risk a fall.
—*Tobias G. Smollett*

Fortune befriends the bold.
—*John Dryden*

Oh courage . . . oh yes! If only one had that . . .
Then life might be livable, in spite of everything.
—*Henrik Ibsen*

But the bravest are surely those who have the clearest
vision of what is before them, glory and danger alike,
and yet notwithstanding go out to meet it.
—*Thucydides*

Courage calls to courage everywhere,
and its voice cannot be denied.
—*Millicent Garrett Fawcett*

———

The courage we desire and prize is not the
courage to die decently, but to live manfully.
—*Thomas Carlyle*

———

Whistling to keep myself from being afraid.
—*John Dryden*

———

If you're scared, just holler and you'll
find it ain't so lonesome out there.
—*Joe Sugden*

———

Have the courage to act instead of react.
—*Earlene Larson Jenks*

———

Brave actions never want a trumpet.
—*English proverb*

The courage of life is often a less
dramatic spectacle than the courage
of a final moment; but it is no less a
magnificent mixture of triumph and tragedy.
A man does what he must—in spite of personal
consequences, in spite of obstacles and dangers and
pressures—and that is the basis of all morality.

—*John F. Kennedy*

No man in the world has more courage
than the man who can stop after eating one peanut.

—*Channing Pollock*

Courage is resistance to fear, mastery
of fear, not absence of fear.

—*Mark Twain*

'Tis not too late tomorrow to be brave.

—*John Armstrong*

I'd rather give my life than be afraid to give it.

—*Lyndon B. Johnson*

Only the brave know how to forgive.
—*Laurence Sterne*

Take courage, my friend, the devil is dead!
—*Charles Reade*

Bravery never goes out of fashion.
—*William Makepeace Thackeray*

It is a lovely thing to live with courage
and die leaving an everlasting renown.
—*Alexander the Great*

The future doesn't belong to the faint-
hearted; it belongs to the brave.
—*Ronald Reagan*

Stand your ground. Don't fire unless fired upon,
but if they mean to have a war let it begin here!
—*John Parker*

Change, Progress & Growth

Progress, therefore, is not an accident,
but a necessity. . . . It is part of nature.

—Herbert Spencer

The need for change bulldozed
a road down the center of my mind.

—Maya Angelou

The improvement of our way of life is more
important than the spreading of it. If we make it
satisfactory enough, it will spread automatically. If we
do not, no strength of arms can permanently oppose it.

—Charles A. Lindbergh

The universe is change; our life
is what our thoughts make it.

—Marcus Aurelius Antoninus

Growth is the only evidence of life.

—Cardinal Newman

We can only change the world by changing men.
—*Charles Wells*

It is hard to let old beliefs go. They are familiar. We are comfortable with them and have spent years building systems and developing habits that depend on them. Like a man who has worn eyeglasses so long that he forgets he has them on, we forget that the world looks to us the way it does because we have become used to seeing it that way through a particular set of lenses. Today, however, we need new lenses. And we need to throw the old ones away.
—*Kenich Ohmae*

All appears to change when we change.
—*Henri Frédéric Amiel*

The good man is the man who, no matter how morally unworthy he has been, is moving to become better.
—*John Dewey*

We must change in order to survive.
—*Pearl Bailey*

We emphasize that we believe in change because
we were born of it, we have lived by it, we prospered
and grew great by it. So the status quo has never been
our god, and we ask no one else to bow down before it.

—*Carl T. Rowan*

Where we cannot invent, we may at least improve.

—*Charles Caleb Colton*

God give us the grace to accept with serenity the
things that cannot be changed; Give us the courage
to change what should be changed; Give us the wisdom
to distinguish one from the other.

—*Reinhold Niebuhr*

Growth demands a temporary surrender of security.

—*Gail Sheehy*

I will keep America moving forward, always
forward—for a better America, for an endless
enduring dream and a thousand points of light.

—*George H. W. Bush*

The world hates change, yet it is the
only thing that has brought progress.
—*Charles F. Kettering*

All growth is a leap in the dark, a spontaneous
unpremeditated act without the benefit of experience.
—*Henry Miller*

Reasonable people adapt themselves to the world.
Unreasonable people attempt to adapt the world
to themselves. All progress, therefore, depends
on unreasonable people.
—*George Bernard Shaw*

Honest disagreement is often a good sign of progress.
—*Gandhi*

Everyone thinks of changing the world,
but no one thinks of changing himself.
—*Leo Tolstoy*

Change is the constant, the signal
for rebirth, the egg of the phoenix.
—*Christina Baldwin*

He that is good, will infallibly become better, and he
that is bad, will as certainly become worse; for vice,
virtue and time are three things that never stand still.
—*Charles Caleb Colton*

Social advance depends as much upon the process
through which it is secured as upon the result itself.
—*Jane Addams*

Things do not change, we do.
—*Henry David Thoreau*

Guard well your spare moments. They are like uncut
diamonds. Discard them and their value will never
be known. Improve them and they will become
the brightest gems in a useful life.
—*Ralph Waldo Emerson*

Those who work most for the world's
advancement are the ones who demand least.
—*Henry Doherty*

Progress lies not in enhancing what is,
but in advancing toward what will be.
—*Kahlil Gibran*

Never believe that a few caring people can't change
the world. For, indeed, that's all who ever have.
—*Margaret Mead*

There is no royal road to anything. One
thing at a time, and all things in succession.
That which grows slowly endures.
—*J. G. Holland*

To die for the revolution is a one-shot deal; to live
for the revolution means taking on the more difficult
commitment of changing our day-to-day life patterns.
—*Frances M. Beal*

The slightest living thing answers a deeper
need than all the works of man because it is
transitory. It has an evanescence of life, or growth,
or change; it passes, as we do, from one stage to
another, from darkness to darkness, into a distance
where we, too, vanish out of sight. A work of art
is static; and its value and its weakness lie in being so:
but the tuft of grass and the clouds above it belong
to our own traveling brotherhood.

—*Freya Stark*

When great changes occur in history, when great
principles are involved, as a rule the majority are wrong.
The minority are usually right.

—*Eugene V. Debs*

Life is either a daring adventure or nothing. To keep
our faces toward change and behave like free spirits
in the presence of fate is strength undefeatable.

—*Helen Keller*

But times do change and move continually.

—*Edmund Spenser*

Reform must come from within, not from without.
You cannot legislate for virtue.
—*James Cardinal Gibbons*

Times don't change. Men do.
—*Sam Levenson*

See everything: overlook a great deal: correct a little.
—*Pope John XXIII*

We must adjust to changing times
and still hold to unchanging principles.
—*Jimmy Carter*

Each new season grows from the leftovers from the past.
That is the essence of change, and change is the basic law.
—*Hal Borland*

The main dangers in this life are the people
who want to change everything . . . or nothing.
—*Lady Nancy Astor*

Why this reluctance to make the change? We fear
the process of reeducation! Adults have invested
endless hours of learning in growing accustomed
to inches and miles; to February's twenty-eight days; to
"night" and "debt" with their silent letters; to qwertyuiop;
and to all the rest. To introduce something altogether new
would mean to begin all over, to become ignorant again,
and to run the old, old risk of failing to learn.

—*Isaac Asimov*

Most new things are not good, and die an early death;
but those which push themselves forward and by slow
degrees force themselves on the attention of mankind
are the unconscious productions of human wisdom,
and must have honest consideration, and must not
be made the subject of unreasoning prejudice.

—*Thomas Brackett Reed*

There is nothing in this world constant, but inconstancy.

—*Jonathan Swift*

Change everything, except your loves.

—*Voltaire*

A permanent state of transition
is man's most noble condition.
—*Juan Ramon Jimenez*

———•———

Turbulence is life force. It is opportunity.
Let's love turbulence and use it for change.
—*Ramsey Clark*

———•———

I will not die an unlived life. I will not live in fear of
falling orcatching fire. I choose to inhabit my days, to
allow my living to open me, to make me less afraid,
more accessible, to loosen my heart until it becomes
a wing, a torch, a promise. I choose to risk my significance; to live so that which comes to me as seed goes
to the next as blossom and that which comes
to me as blossom, goes on as fruit.
—*Dawna Markova*

———•———

We must lighten ourselves to survive. We must
not cling. Safety lies in lessening, in becoming
random and thin enough for the new to enter.
—*John Updike*

Guard well your spare moments. They are like uncut
diamonds. Discard them and their value will never
be known. Improve them and they will become
the brightest gems in a useful life.

—*Ralph Waldo Emerson*

I am telling young people that if you're dissatisfied
with the way things are . . . get out there and occupy
these positions in government and make the decisions.

—*Barbara Jordan*

When people made up their minds that they wanted
to be free and took action, then there was change.

—*Rosa Parks*

The things I don't like, I will try to change.

—*Medger Evers*

Where there is hope there is life, where there is life there is
possibility, and where there is possibility change can occur.

—*Jesse Jackson*

When you plant lettuce, if it does not grow well, you don't blame the lettuce. You look for reasons it is not doing well. It may need fertilizer, or more water, or less sun. You never blame the lettuce. Yet if we have problems with our friends or family, we blame the other person. But if we know how to take care of them, they will grow well, like the lettuce. Blaming has no positive effect at all, nor does trying to persuade using reason and argument. That is my experience. No blame, no reasoning, no argument, just understanding. If you understand, and you show that you understand, you can love, and the situation will change.

—*Thich Nhat Hanh*

The spirit of self-help is the root of all genuine growth in the individual; and, exhibited in the lives of many, it constitutes the true source of national vigor and strength.

—*Samuel Smiles*

The more things change, the more they stay the same.

—*Alphonse Karr*

The place to improve the world is first in one's own heart and head and hands.

—*Robert M. Pirsig*

Movement is the magic which keeps
expectations high in America.
—*James Oliver Robertson*

What you do
Still betters what is done.
—*William Shakespeare*

And from the discontent of man
The world's best progress springs.
—*Ella Wheeler Wilcox*

Change is inevitable. In a progressive
country change is constant.
—*Benjamin Disraeli*

Why stay we on the earth except to grow?
—*Robert Browning*

There is nothing permanent except change.
—*Heraclitus*

When we blindly adopt a religion, a political system, a literary dogma, we become automatons. We cease to grow.
—*Anaïs Nin*

Life belongs to the living, and he who lives must be prepared for changes.
—*Johann Wolfgang von Goethe*

There's only one corner of the universe you can be certain of improving and that's your own self.
—*Aldous Huxley*

There are many ways of going forward, but only one way of standing still.
—*Franklin D. Roosevelt*

Courage is the price that Life exacts for granting peace.
—*Amelia Earhart*

Character & Personality

Character is higher than intellect.
—*Ralph Waldo Emerson*

Character is what God and the angels know of us;
reputation is what men and women think of us.
—*Horace Mann*

Nearly all men can stand adversity, but if you
want to test a man's character, give him power.
—*Abraham Lincoln*

If you have anything really valuable to contribute to the
world it will come through the expression of your own
personality, that single spark of divinity that sets you off
and makes you different from every other living creature.
—*Bruce Barton*

You can't guarantee being born a Lord. It is impossible—
you've shown it—to be born a gentleman.
—*Harold Wilson*

First find the man in yourself if you
will inspire manliness in others.
—*Amos Bronson Alcott*

A lady is one who never shows
her underwear unintentionally.
—*Lillian Day*

A gentleman should be able to play
the flute, but not too expertly.
—*Aristotle*

Let us not say, Every man is the architect
of his own fortune; but let us say, Every man
is the architect of his own character.
—*George Dana Boardman*

The real character of a man is
found out by his amusements.
—*Joshua Reynolds*

Personality is to a man what perfume is to a flower.
—*Charles M. Schwab*

More is a man of angel's wit and singular learning;
I know not his fellow. For where is the man of that
gentleness, lowliness and affability? And as time requireth,
a man of marvelous mirth and pastimes; and sometimes
of as sad a gravity: as who say a man for all seasons.
—*Robert Whittington*

Characters do not change. Opinions alter,
but characters are only developed.
—*Benjamin Disraeli*

The true test of character is not how much
we know how to do, but how we behave
when we don't know what to do.
—*John Holt*

We want the spirit of America to be efficient; we
want American character to be efficient; we want
American character to display itself in what may,
perhaps, be allowed to call spiritual efficiency—
clear disinterested thinking and fearless action
along the right lines of thought.
—*Woodrow Wilson*

This would be said of me:
he loved children, cats and dogs,
and beauty in all its guises—
a face, a figure, picture and poem
and the texture and colour of clouds;
not afraid of the verb "to love"
and the use of it, sometimes perhaps
too often, and sometimes not enough,
but always with meaning at the same time.
He suffered the pains of the world,
blunderingly trying to remedy them.
He could forgive others more easily
than he could forgive himself.
He tried hard in all his endeavours,
and lamented that he lost the game,
but enjoyed playing it; and lastly,
he was at all times aware of God.

—*Vernon Noble*

Character isn't inherited. One builds it daily by the
way one thinks and acts, thought by thought, action
by action. If one lets fear or hate or anger take possession of the mind, they become self-forged chains.

—*Helen Gahagan Douglas*

Nature says to a woman: "Be beautiful if you can,
wise if you want to, but be respected—that is essential."
—*Beaumarchais*

He was the very pineapple of politeness!
—*Richard Brinsley Sheridan*

You must look into people, as well as at them.
—*Lord Chesterfield*

One's eyes are what one is,
one's mouth what one becomes.
—*John Galsworthy*

Character cannot be developed in ease and quiet. Only
through experience of trial and suffering can the soul
be strengthened, ambition inspired, and success achieved.
—*Helen Keller*

To measure the man, measure his heart.
—*Malcolm Stevenson Forbes*

I'm the foe of moderation, the champion of excess. If I may lift a line from a die-hard whose identity is lost in the shuffle, "I'd rather be strongly wrong than weakly right."
—*Tallulah Bankhead*

Make the most of yourself, for that is all there is of you.
—*Ralph Waldo Emerson*

During my eighty-seven years I have witnessed a whole succession of technological revolutions. But none of them has done away with the need for character in the individual or the ability to think.
—*Bernard Baruch*

I am better than my reputation.
—*Friedrich von Schiller*

The four cornerstones of character on which the structure of this nation was built are: Initiative, Imagination, Individuality, and Independence.
—*Edward Rickenbacker*

Bald as the bare mountain tops are bald,
 with a baldness full of grandeur.
—*Matthew Arnold*

We should take care not to make the intellect our god;
it has, of course, powerful muscles, but no personality.
—*Albert Einstein*

The character of human life, like the character
of the human condition, like the character of all life,
is "ambiguity": the inseparable mixture of good and
evil, the true and false, the creative and destructive
forces—both individual and social.
—*Paul Tillich*

Clothes and manners do not make the man; but,
when he is made, they greatly improve his appearance.
—*Henry Ward Beecher*

Man becomes man only by the intelligence,
 but he is man only by the heart.
—*Henri Frédéric Amiel*

A good heart is better than all the heads in the world.
—*Edward Bulwer-Lytton*

There is a passion for hunting something
deeply implanted in the human breast.
—*Charles Dickens*

There is no such thing as a "self-made" man. We are
made up of thousands of others. Everyone who has
ever done a kind deed for us, or spoken one word of
encouragement to us, has entered into the make-up of
our character and of our thoughts, as well as our successes.
—*George Matthew Adams*

They are never alone that are
accompanied with noble thoughts.
—*Sir Philip Sidney*

If you want to be witty, work on your character
and say what you think on every occasion.
—*Stendhal*

Sports do not build character. They reveal it.
—*Heywood Hale Broun*

Decency—generosity—cooperation—assistance in trouble—devotion to duty; these are the things that are of greater value than surface appearances and customs.
—*Dwight D. Eisenhower*

Many people have character who have nothing else.
—*Don Herold*

The best index to a person's character is (a) how he treats people who can't do him any good, and (b) how he treats people who can't fight back.
—*Abigail van Buren*

We do not believe in ourselves until someone reveals that deep inside us is valuable, worth listening to, worthy of our trust, sacred to our touch. Once we believe in ourselves we can risk curiosity, wonder, spontaneous delight or any experience that reveals the human spirit.
—*e. e. cummings*

Enthusiasm is the greatest asset in the world.
It beats money and power and influence.
—*Henry Chester*

If I take care of my character, my
reputation will take care of itself.
—*D. L. Moody*

If you think about what you ought to do for
other people, your character will take care of itself.
—*Woodrow Wilson*

You cannot dream yourself into a character;
you must hammer and forge yourself one.
—*James A. Froude*

Character is that which can do without success.
—*Ralph Waldo Emerson*

He was not of an age but for all time.
—*Ben Jonson*

Manners maketh man.
—*William of Wykeham*

Practice yourself what you preach.
—*Titus Maccius Plautus*

Neither will I make myself anybody's laughing-stock.
—*Miguel de Cervantes*

The good have no need of an advocate.
—*Phocion*

Bad men live that they may eat and drink,
whereas good men eat and drink that they may live.
—*Socrates*

Sow a thought, and you reap an act;
Sow an act, and you reap a habit;
Sow a habit, and you reap a character;
Sow a character, and you reap a destiny.
—*Charles Reade*

Leadership involves conduct. Conduct is determined
by values. Values are what makes us who we are.
—*General H. Norman Schwarzkopf*

———•———

Character is a perfectly educated will.
—*Novalis*

———•———

In thy face I see
The map of honor, truth, and loyalty.
—*William Shakespeare*

———•———

To enjoy the things we ought and to hate the things we
ought has the greatest bearing on excellence of character.
—*Aristotle*

———•———

No evil can happen to a good man,
either in life or after death.
—*Plato*

———•———

We must have richness of soul.
—*Antiphanes*

Never has a man who has bent himself
been able to make others straight.

—*Mencius*

None but the well-bred man knows how to confess
a fault, or acknowledge himself in an error.

—*Benjamin Franklin*

So faithful in love, and so dauntless in war,
There never was a knight like the young Lochinvar.

—*Sir Walter Scott*

To err is human, to forgive is divine.

—*Alexander Pope*

Were I so tall to reach the pole,
Or grasp the ocean with my span,
I must be measured by my soul;
The mind's the standard of the man.

—*Isaac Watts*

Every man has to seek in his own way to make his own
self more noble and to realize his own true worth.
—*Albert Schweitzer*

But if it be a sin to covet honor,
I am the most offending soul alive.
—*William Shakespeare*

A man has a right to be judged by how he acts,
not by how someone may have told you he acts.
—*Allan W. Eckert*

The tendency of a man's nature to good is like
the tendency of water to flow downwards.
—*Mencius*

Her angel's face
As the great eye of heaven shined bright,
And made a sunshine in the shady place.
—*Edmund Spenser*

Will is to grace as the horse is to the rider.

—*St. Augustine*

No, when the fight begins within himself,
A man's worth something.

—*Robert Browning*

Noble be man,
Helpful and good!
For that alone
Sets him apart
From every other creature
On earth.

—*Johann Wolfgang von Goethe*

Be valiant, but not too venturous. Let
thy attire be comely, but not costly.

—*John Lyly*

Where my heart lies, let my brain lie also.

—*Robert Browning*

What lies behind us and what lies before us are
tiny matters compared to what lies within us.
—*Oliver Wendell Holmes*

I keep my ideals, because in spite of everything,
I still believe that people are really good at heart.
—*Anne Frank*

A noble person attracts noble people,
and knows how to hold on to them.
—*Johann Wolfgang von Goethe*

Children & Youth

Give a little love to a child, and you get a great deal back.
—*John Ruskin*

———•———

Backward, turn backward, O Time, in your flight,
Make me a child again just for one night.
—*Elizabeth Akers Allen*

———•———

No one has yet fully realized the wealth of sympathy, kindness and generosity hidden in the soul of the child.
—*Emma Goldman*

———•———

We wove a web in childhood,
A web of sunny air.
—*Charlotte Brontë*

———•———

If you have a great passion it seems that the logical thing is to see the fruit of it, and the fruit are children.
—*Roman Polanski*

Babies are such a nice way to start people.
—Don Herold

When the first baby laughed for the first time, the laugh broke into a thousand pieces and they all went skipping about, and that was the beginning of fairies.
—James Matthew Barrie

A child becomes an adult when he realizes that he has a right not only to be right but also to be wrong.
—Thomas Szasz

To grown people a girl of fifteen and a half is a child still; to herself she is very old and very real; more real, perhaps, than ever before.
—Margaret Widdemer

Youths have a tremendous advantage over their elders in possessing the power of vision without the drawback of retrospect.
—Henry Ford

When a child is born, so are grandmothers.
—*Judith Levy*

Life would be infinitely happier if we could only be born
at the age of eighty and gradually approach eighteen.
—*Mark Twain*

Young people are in a condition like permanent intoxica-
tion, because youth is sweet and they are growing.
—*Aristotle*

The best way to make children
good is to make them happy.
—*Oscar Wilde*

Children are our most valuable resource.
—*Herbert Hoover*

On with the dance! let joy be unconfined;
No sleep till morn, when Youth and Pleasure meet
To chase the glowing hours with flying feet.
—*Lord Byron*

I am not young enough to know everything.

—*Oscar Wilde*

The potential possibilities of any child are the
most intriguing and stimulating in all creation.

—*Ray L. Wilbur*

The confidence of the young is truly remarkable.

—*Lucille Ball*

In every child who is born, under no matter what
circumstances, and of no matter what parents, the
potentiality of the human race is born again.

—*James Agee*

Childhood Is the Kingdom Where Nobody Dies.

—*Edna St. Vincent Millay*

I no longer think that what two-
year-olds say is nonsense.

—*George Will*

We need the enthusiasm of the young. We need their *joie de vivre*. In it is reflected something of the original joy God had in creating man. The young experience this same joy within themselves. This joy is the same everywhere, but it is also ever new and original. The young know how to express this joy in their own special way.

—*Pope John Paul II*

The young do not know enough to be prudent, and therefore they attempt the impossible—and achieve it, generation after generation.

—*Pearl S. Buck*

A young man must let his ideas grow, not be continually rooting them up to see how they are getting on.

—*William McFee*

If help and salvation are to come, they can only come from the children, for the children are the makers of men.

—*Maria Montessori*

Youth has no age.

—*Pablo Picasso*

The great man is he who does not lose his child's-heart.
—*Mencius*

Fortunately for us and our world, youth is not easily discouraged. Youth with its clear vista and boundless faith and optimism is uninhibited by the thousands of considerations that always bedevil man in his progress. The hopes of the world rest on the flexibility, vigor, capacity for new thought, and the fresh outlook of the young.
—*Dwight D. Eisenhower*

Young people should remain idealistic all their lives. If you have to choose between being Don Quixote and Sancho Panza, for heaven's sake, be the Don.
—*Ramsey Clark*

The pursuit of happiness, which American citizens are obliged to undertake, tends to involve them in trying to perpetuate the moods, tastes and aptitudes of youth.
—*Malcolm Muggeridge*

Though she be but little, she is fierce.
—*William Shakespeare*

If a child is to keep alive his inborn sense of wonder,
he needs the companionship of at least one adult who
can share it, rediscovering with him the joy, excitement
and mystery of the world we live in.

—*Rachel Carson*

In early youth, as we contemplate our coming
life, we are like children in a theatre before
the curtain is raised, sitting there in high spirits
and eagerly waiting for the play to begin.

—*Arthur Schopenhauer*

Youth has one great element in its favor—
it can live in the future.

—*Henry Ford*

No man of my generation has any business to address
youth unless he comes to the task not in the spirit of
exultation, but in a spirit of humility.

—*Franklin D. Roosevelt*

It takes a long time to become young.

—*Pablo Picasso*

O Youth: Do you know that yours is not the first
generation to yearn for a life of beauty and freedom?
Do you know that all your ancestors felt as you do—
and fell victim to trouble and hatred? Do you know,
also, that your fervent wishes can only find fulfillment
if you succeed in attaining love and understanding of
men and animals, and plants, and stars, so that every
joy becomes your joy and every pain your pain?
Open your eyes, your heart, your hands, and avoid the
poison your forebears so greedily sucked in from History.
Then will all the earth be your fatherland, and all
your work and effort spread forth blessings.

—*Albert Einstein*

The highlight of my childhood was making my
brother laugh so hard that food came out of his nose.

—*Garrison Keillor*

The younger generation will come knocking at my door.

—*Henrik Ibsen*

A baby is God's opinion that the world should go on.

—*Carl Sandburg*

So nigh is grandeur to our dust,
So near is God to man,
When Duty whispers low, Thou must,
The youth replies, I can.
—*Ralph Waldo Emerson*

The number-one thing young people in America—
indeed, young people around the world—have going
for them is their sense of honesty, morality, and ethics.
Young people refuse to accept the lies and
rationalizations of the established order.
—*Dick Gregory*

I do not know what I may appear to the world; but to
myself I seem to have been only like a boy playing on
the seashore, and diverting myself in now and then finding
a smoother pebble or a prettier shell than ordinary, whilst
the great ocean of truth lay all undiscovered before me.
—*Sir Isaac Newton*

Age does not make us childish, as they say.
It only finds us true children still.
—*Johann Wolfgang von Goethe*

If I can leave a single message with the younger
generation, it is to lash yourself to the mast, like
Ulysses if you must, to escape the siren calls
of complacency and indifference.

—*Edward M. Kennedy*

All kids need is a little help, a little hope,
and somebody who believes in them.

—*Earvin (Magic) Johnson*

Children ask better questions than do adults. "May I
have a cookie?" "Why is the sky blue?" and "What does
a cow say?" are far more likely to elicit a cheerful response
than "Where's your manuscript?" "Why haven't you
called?" and "Who's your lawyer?"

—*Fran Lebowitz*

It's a family joke that when I was a tiny child,
I turned from the window out of which I was watching
a snowstorm, and hopefully asked, "Momma, do
we believe in winter?"

—*Philip Roth*

There are two lasting bequests we can hope to give
our children: One of these is roots. The other, wings.
—*Hodding Carter, Jr.*

Our greatest natural resource
is the minds of our children.
—*Walt Disney*

Bliss was it in that dawn to be alive,
But to be young was very heaven!
—*William Wordsworth*

Children's talent to endure stems
from their ignorance of alternatives
—*Maya Angelou*

Grown-ups never understand anything for
themselves, and it is tiresome for children to be
always and forever explaining things to them.
—*Antoine de Saint Exupéry*

If you make children happy now, you will make them
happy twenty years hence by the memory of it.
—*Kate Douglas Wiggin*

Sweet childish days, that were as long
As twenty days are now.
—*William Wordsworth*

Nothing you do for children is ever wasted. They seem not
to notice us, hovering, averting our eyes, and they seldom
offer thanks, but what we do for them is never wasted.
—*Garrison Keillor*

A child loves his play, not because
it's easy, but because it's hard.
—*Benjamin Spock*

Criticism

If you criticize a mule, do it to his face.
—*Herbert V. Prochnow*

To avoid criticism, do nothing, say nothing, and be nothing.
—*Elbert Hubbard*

The readiest and surest way to get rid
of censure, is to correct ourselves.
—*Demosthenes*

Criticism, as it was first instituted by Aristotle,
was meant as a standard of judging well.
—*Samuel Johnson*

It is folly for an eminent man to think of escaping
censure, and a weakness to be affected with it. All the
illustrious persons of antiquity, and indeed of every age
in the world, have passed through this fiery persecution.
—*Joseph Addison*

Give the world the best you have
and you might get kicked in the teeth.
Give the world the best you've got anyway.
—*Mother Teresa*

Remember that nobody will ever get ahead of you
as long as he is kicking you in the seat of the pants.
—*Walter Winchell*

He who would acquire fame must not show himself afraid
of censure. The dread of censure is the death of genius.
—*William Gilmore Simms*

Do not attempt to do a thing unless you
are sure of yourself; but do not relinquish it simply
because someone else is not sure of you.
—*Stewart E. White*

Critics are like eunuchs in a harem: they know
how it's done, they've see it done every day,
but they're unable to do it themselves.
—*Brendan Behan*

Candor is the brightest gem of criticism.
—*Benjamin Disraeli*

I was brought up to believe that how I saw myself
was more important than how others saw me.
—*Anwar el-Sadat*

The censure of those who are opposed to us,
is the highest commendation that can be given us.
—*Seigneur de Saint-Evremond*

Unless the bastards have the courage to give
you unqualified praise, I say ignore them.
—*John Steinbeck*

A bad review is even less important than
whether it is raining in Patagonia.
—*Iris Murdoch*

It is better to be looked over than overlooked.
—*Mae West*

Illegitimis non carborundum.
(Don't let the bastards grind you down.)
—*Joseph Stilwell*

A fly, Sir, may sting a stately horse and make him wince;
but one is but an insect, and the other a horse still.
—*Samuel Johnson*

The public is the only critic whose
opinion is worth anything at all.
—*Mark Twain*

If Jesus Christ were to come today, people would not
even crucify him. They would ask him to dinner, and
hear what he had to say, and make fun of him.
—*Thomas Carlyle*

When I stopped being prisoner to what I worried was
others' opinions of me, I became more confident and free.
—*Lucille Ball*

Criticism is a misconception: we must read not
to understand others but to understand ourselves.
—*E. M. Cioran*

The worse the press, the better.
—*Eddie van Halen*

Any fool can criticize, and many of them do.
—*Archbishop C. Garbett*

He who flings dirt at another dirtieth himself most.
—*Thomas Fuller*

Everything I did in my life that
was worthwhile I caught hell for.
—*Earl Warren*

No one can make you feel inferior without your consent.
—*Eleanor Roosevelt*

How much quicker we are to find fault and speak of what annoys us than of that which is pleasant and cheerful. How much plainer people's faults show than their virtues.

—*Mary Jane Mount Tanner*

Pay no attention to what the critics say;
no statue has ever been erected to a critic.

—*Jean Sibelius*

He has a right to criticize, who has a heart to help.

—*Abraham Lincoln*

When critics disagree, the artist is in accord with himself.

—*Oscar Wilde*

It is much easier to be critical than to be correct.

—*Benjamin Disraeli*

Those serpents! There's no pleasing them!

—*Lewis Carroll*

Determination

In the lexicon of youth, which fate reserves
For a bright manhood, there is no such word
As "fail."
—*Edward Robert Bulwer-Lytton*

It's not as though we're especially gifted.
We may have been lucky—even that, I don't know
about—but we have been exceptionally determined.
—*Jerry Garcia*

It's not the size of the dog in the fight,
but the size of the fight in the dog.
—*Mark Twain*

Some say that the age of chivalry is past, that the
spirit of romance is dead. The age of chivalry is never
past, so long as there is a wrong left unredressed on
earth, or a man or woman left to say, I will redress
that wrong, or spend my life in the attempt.
—*Charles Kingsley*

The greatest intellectual capacities are only found in
connection with a vehement and passionate will.
—*Arthur Schopenhauer*

Obstacles don't have to stop you. If you run
into a wall, don't turn around and give up. Figure
out how to climb it, go through it, or work around it.
—*Michael Jordan*

The weakest kind of fruit
Drops earliest to the ground.
—*William Shakespeare*

We are adhering to life now with
our last muscle—the heart.
—*Djuna Barnes*

You may break, you may shatter the vase, if you will.
But the scent of roses will hang round it still.
—*Thomas Moore*

Education

Teaching kids to count is fine,
but teaching them what counts is best.
—*Bob Talbert*

Give instruction to a wise man, and he will be still wiser.
Teach a righteous man, and he will increase his learning.
—*adapted from Proverbs 9:9*

To endure is the first thing that a child ought to learn,
and that which he will have the most need to know.
—*Jean-Jacques Rousseau*

A man can only attain knowledge with the help of those
who possess it. This must be understood from the very
beginning. One must learn from him who knows.
—*George Gurdjieff*

Education is a better safeguard
of liberty than a standing army.
—*Edward Everett*

You cannot teach a man anything; you can
only help him find it within himself.

—*Galileo*

The brighter you are the more you have to learn.

—*Don Herold*

The wisest man has something yet to learn.

—*George Santayana*

A school is not a factory. Its raison d'etre
is to provide opportunity for experience.

—*J. L. Carr*

The teacher is one who makes two ideas
grow where only one grew before.

—*Elbert Hubbard*

One good schoolmaster is worth a thousand priests.

—*Robert Green Ingersoll*

If we mean to have heroes, statesmen and philosophers, we should have learned women.... If much depends as is allowed upon the early education of youth and the first principles which are instilled take the deepest root, great benefit must arise from literary accomplishments in women.

—Abigail Adams

Education in the long run is an affair that works itself out between the individual student and his opportunities. Methods of which we talk so much play but a minor part. Offer the opportunities, leave the student to his natural reaction on them, and he will work out his personal destiny, be it a high one or a low one.

—William James

There is only one sound method of moral education. It is teaching people to think.

—Everett Dean Martin

Educated men are as much superior to uneducated men as the living are to the dead.

—Aristotle

The man who can make hard things easier is the educator.
—*Ralph Waldo Emerson*

Real education must ultimately be limited to men
who insist on knowing, the rest is mere sheepherding.
—*Ezra Pound*

Our children must be knowledgeable. They must be
literate in the language of the twenty-first century. They
must be ready to compete. They must be challenged to
be the very best students they can be. And we must never
leave any child behind by pushing him forward. I refuse
to give up on any child, and that is why I argue so
passionately against social promotion.
—*George W. Bush*

A good education should leave much to be desired.
—*Alan Gregg*

Education is to get where you can start to learn.
—*George Aiken*

He who won't be counseled can't be helped.
—*Benjamin Franklin*

Our lives teach us who we are.
—*Sulman Rushdie*

[They] realized that education was not a thing of
one's own to do with what one pleases—that it was
not a personal privilege to be merely enjoyed by the pos-
sessor—but a precious treasure transmitted; a sacred trust
to be held, used and enjoyed, and if possible strengthened—then passed on to others upon the same trust.
—*Louis D. Brandeis*

To teach is to learn twice.
—*Joseph Joubert*

Education and work are the levers to uplift a
people. Work alone will not do it unless inspired
by the right ideals and guided by intelligence.
Education must not teach work—it must teach life.
—*W. E. B. Du Bois*

The mind is like the stomach. It is not how much
you put into it that counts, but how much it digests.
—*Albert Jay Nock*

The acceptance of women as authority figures or
as role models is an important step in female education. . . . It is this process of identification, respect,
and then self-respect that promotes growth.
—*Judy Chicago*

Respect for the fragility and importance of an individual
life is still the first mark of the educated man.
—*Norman Cousins*

Education has become too
important to be left to educators.
—*Peter F. Drucker*

To learn is to change. Education
is a process that changes the learner.
—*George B. Leonard*

All education is a continuous dialogue—questions
and answers that pursue every problem to the horizon.
That is the essence of academic freedom.
—*William O. Douglas*

Education is that which remains, if one
has forgotten everything he learned in school.
—*Albert Einstein*

It is the trained, living human soul, cultivated
and strengthened by long study and thought, that
breathes the real breath of life into boys and girls
and makes them human, whether they be black
or white, Greek, Russian, or American.
—*W. E. B. Du Bois*

Sit down before fact as a little child, be prepared to give up
every preconceived notion, follow humbly wherever and
to whatever abyss nature leads, or you shall learn nothing.
—*Thomas Huxley*

No man ever prayed heartily without learning something.
—*Ralph Waldo Emerson*

Life is amazing: and the teacher had better prepare
himself to be a medium for that amazement.
—*Edward Blishen*

———

There is no real teacher who in practice does
not believe in the existence of the soul, or
in a magic that acts on it through speech.
—*Allan Bloom*

———

Education is a private matter between the
person and the world of knowledge and experience,
and has little to do with school or college.
—*Lillian Smith*

———

The aim of [education] must be the training of independ-
ently acting and thinking individuals, who, however, see in
the service of the community their highest life problem.
—*Albert Einstein*

———

If you educate a man, you educate a person,
but if you educate a woman, you educate a family.
—*Ruby Manikan*

Liberty without learning is always in peril
and learning without liberty is always in vain.
—*John F. Kennedy*

———

Education is the ability to listen to almost anything
without losing your temper or your self-confidence.
—*Robert Frost*

———

The ability to think straight, some knowledge
of the past, some vision of the future, some skill
to do useful service, some urge to fit that service into
the well-being of the community—these are the most
vital things education must try to produce.
—*Virginia Gildersleeve*

———

Only the educated are free.

—*Epictetus*

———

I took a good deal o' pains with his eddication, sir; let
him run in the streets when he was very young, and shift
for hisself. It's the only way to make a boy sharp, sir.
—*Charles Dickens*

It's what you learn after you know it all that counts.

—*John Wooden*

Our progress as a nation can be no swifter
than our progress in education. . . . The human
mind is our fundamental resource.

—*John F. Kennedy*

A child educated only at school is an uneducated child.

—*George Santayana*

A man should keep his little brain attic stocked
with all the furniture that he is likely to use, and
the rest he can put away in the lumber-room
of the library, where he can get it if he wants it.

—*Arthur Conan Doyle*

Whenever a person gets too big to study,
he is as big as he ever will be.

—*Herbert V. Prochnow*

The learned is happy, nature to explore,
The fool is happy, that he knows no more.
—*Alexander Pope*

Real education should educate us out of self
into something far finer—into selflessness
which links us with all humanity.
—*Lady Nancy Astor*

Education is the best provision for old age.
—*Aristotle*

The best education in the world is
that by struggling to get a living.
—*Wendell Phillips*

Bear in mind that the wonderful things you learn in
your schools are the work of many generations. All this
is put in your hands as your inheritance in order that
you may receive it, honor it, add to it, and one day
faithfully hand it on to your children.
—*Albert Einstein*

I would live to study, not study to live.
—*Francis Bacon*

If you think education is expensive—try ignorance.
—*Derek Bok*

Education is not the filling of a pail,
but the lighting of a fire.
—*William Butler Yeats*

We can learn even from our enemies.
—*Ovid*

Learning makes a man fit company for himself.
—*Thomas Fuller*

I forget what I was taught. I only remember what
I have learned.
—*Patrick White*

I never let my schooling interfere with my education.
—*Mark Twain*

Education makes people easy to lead, but difficult
to drive; easy to govern, but impossible to enslave.
—*Henry Peter Brougham*

Education should be gentle and stern, not cold and lax.
—*Joseph Joubert*

Education has for its object the formation of character.
—*Herbert Spencer*

What is the first part of politics? Education. The second?
Education. And the third? Education.
—*Jules Michelet*

Education is that which discloses to the wise and
disguises from the foolish their lack of understanding.
—*Ambrose Bierce*

Education is too important to be
left solely to the educators.
—*Francis Keppel*

I am not willing that this discussion should close
without mention of the value of a true teacher. Give
me a log hut, with only a simple bench, Mark Hopkins
on one end and I on the other, and you may have all
the buildings, apparatus and libraries without him.
—*James A. Garfield*

To make your children capable of
honesty is the beginning of education.
—*John Ruskin*

Education costs money, but then so does ignorance.
—*Claus Moser*

A good education is not so much one which
prepares a man to succeed in the world, as one
which enables him to sustain failure.
—*Bernard Iddings Bell*

Real education should educate us out of self
into something far finer; into a selflessness
which links us with all humanity.
—*Lady Nancy Astor*

The test and the use of man's education is that
he finds pleasure in the exercise of his mind.
—*Jacques Barzun*

A teacher affects eternity; he can
never tell where his influence stops.
—*Henry Adams*

Learning is not attained by chance, it must be sought
for with ardor and attended to with diligence.
—*Abigail Adams*

But since we are all likely to go astray,
The reasonable thing is to learn from those who can teach.
—*Sophocles*

He who opens a school door, closes a prison.
—*Victor Hugo*

The very spring and root of honesty
and virtue lie in good education.
—*Plutarch*

The liberally educated person is one who is able to resist
the easy and preferred answers, not because he is obstinate,
but because he knows others worthy of consideration.

—Allan Bloom

The direction in which education starts
a man will determine his future life.

—Plato

Eduacation is not the filling of the pail,
but the lighting of a fire.

—William Butler Yeats

Effort & Labor

The harder you work, the luckier you get.
—Gary Player

Work and love—these are the basics.
Without them there is neurosis.
—Theodor Reik

Choose a job you love and you'll never
have to work a day in your life.
—Confucius

Attempt the impossible in order to improve your work.
—Bette Davis

Continuous effort—not strength or intelligence
—is the key to unlocking our potential.
—Liane Cordes

It is better to wear out than to rust out.
—George Whitefield

It is hard to fail, but it is worse never to have tried
to succeed. In this life we get nothing save by effort.
—*Theodore Roosevelt*

The men and women who have the right
ideals ... are those who have the courage to strive
for the happiness which comes only with labor and
effort and self-sacrifice, and those who join in life springs
in part from power of work and sense of duty.
—*Theodore Roosevelt*

There is no genius in life like the
genius of energy and industry.
—*Donald Grant Mitchell*

Work is the inevitable condition of human life,
the true source of human welfare.
—*Leo Tolstoy*

Talent is cheaper than table salt. What separates the talented
individual from the successful one is a lot of hard work.
—*Stephen King*

A man is a worker. If he is not that he is nothing.
—*Joseph Conrad*

Work is the meat of life, pleasure the dessert.
—*Bertie Charles Forbes*

Labor is man's greatest function. He is nothing,
he can do nothing, he can achieve nothing,
he can fulfill nothing, without working.
—*Orville Dewey*

Work is the greatest thing in the world, so
we should always save some of it for tomorrow.
—*Don Herold*

There is no real wealth but the labor of man.
—*Percy Bysshe Shelley*

Loyal and efficient work in a great cause, even though it
may not be immediately recognized, ultimately bears fruit.
—*Jawaharlal Nehru*

It is only through labor and painful effort, by grim energy
and resolute courage, that we move on to better things.
—*Theodore Roosevelt*

The expectations of life depend upon
diligence; the mechanic that would perfect
his work must first sharpen his tools.
—*Confucius*

Everything comes to him who hustles while he waits.
—*Thomas A. Edison*

The only method by which people can be supported
is out of the effort of those who are earning their own
way. We must not create a deterrent to hard work.
—*Robert A. Taft*

Excellence in any department can be attained
only by the labor of a lifetime; it is not to be
purchased at a lesser price.
—*Samuel Johnson*

No person who is enthusiastic about his
work has anything to fear from life.
—*Samuel Goldwyn*

He who labors diligently need never despair;
for all things are accomplished by diligence and labor.
—*Menander of Athens*

The fruit derived from labor is the sweetest of all pleasures.
—*Luc de Clapiers*

Life grants nothing to us mortals without hard work.
—*Horace*

God gives every bird his worm, but
He does not throw it into the nest.
—*P. D. James*

Work banishes those three great evils,
boredom, vice and poverty.
—*Voltaire*

Things don't turn up in this world
until somebody turns them up.
—*James A. Garfield*

I don't suppose that hard work, discipline, and a
perfectionist attitude toward my work did me any harm.
—*Lucille Ball*

Nothing ever comes to one that is worth
having, except as a result of hard work.
—*Booker T. Washington*

Rome was not built in one day.
—*John Heywood*

For it is commonly said: accomplished labours are pleasant.
—*Marcus Tullius Cicero*

Amateurs hope. Professionals work.
—*Garson Kanin*

It is no use saying, "We are doing our best."
You have got to succeed in doing what is necessary.
—*Winston Churchill*

The world is full of willing people; some willing
to work, the rest willing to let them.
—*Robert Frost*

It's the constant and determined effort that breaks
down resistance, sweeps away all obstacles.
—*Claude M. Bristol*

The only place where success comes
before work is in a dictionary.
—*Vidal Sassoon*

It's not the hours you put in your work that
counts, it's the work you put in the hours.
—*Sam Ewing*

We work to become, not to acquire.
—*Elbert Hubbard*

To love what you do and feel that it
matters—how could anything be more fun?
—*Katherine Graham*

As a remedy against all ills—poverty, sickness,
and melancholy—only one thing is absolutely
necessary: a liking for work.
—*Charles Bauldelaire*

Honest labor bears a lovely face.
—*Thomas Dekker*

The Gods rank work above virtues.
—*Hesiod*

The secret of the truly successful, I believe, is that they
learned very early in life how not to be busy.
They saw through that adage, repeated to me so often in
childhood, that anything worth doing is worth doing well.
The truth is, many things are worth doing only in the
most slovenly, halfhearted fashion possble, and many
other things are not worth doing at all.
—*Barbara Ehrenreich*

Equality

If you want to make beautiful music, you must
play the black and the white notes together.
—*Richard Nixon*

We hold these truths to be self-evident,
that all men are created equal.
—*Thomas Jefferson*

We must learn to live together as
brothers or perish together as fools.
—*Martin Luther King, Jr.*

Equal opportunity means everyone will
have a fair chance at being incompetent.
—*Laurence J. Peter*

The Constitution does not provide
for first and second class citizens.
—*Wendell Willkie*

All animals are equal, but some are more equal than others.
—George Orwell

When white and black and brown and every other color
decide they're going to live together as Christians, then and
only then are we going to see an end to these troubles.
—Barry M. Goldwater

The most certain test by which we judge whether
a country is really free is the amount of security
enjoyed by minorities.
—Lord Acton

I have a dream that my four little children will one day
live in a nation where they will not be judged by the
color of their skin but by the content of their character.
—Martin Luther King, Jr.

Fourscore and seven years ago our fathers brought forth
on this continent, a new nation, conceived in Liberty, and
dedicated to the proposition that all men are created equal.
—Abraham Lincoln

It is our duty to make sure that, big as this country is,
there is no room for racial or religious intolerance—
and that there is no room for snobbery.

—*Franklin D. Roosevelt*

Equality of opportunity is an equal
opportunity to prove unequal talents.

—*Viscount Samuel*

Our Constitution is color-blind, and neither knows
nor tolerates classes among citizens. In respect of
civil rights, all citizens are equal before the law. The
humblest is the peer of the most powerful.

—*John Marshall Harlan*

The struggle for equal opportunity in America is the
struggle for America's soul. The ugliness of bigotry stands
in direct contradiction to the very meaning of America.

—*Hubert H. Humphrey*

It is never too late to give up our prejudices.

—*Henry David Thoreau*

All human beings are born free
and equal in dignity and rights.
—Anonymous

Universal Declaration of Human Rights (1948) article 1:
Choose equality.
—Matthew Arnold

Men are equal; it is not birth
but virtue that makes the difference.
—Voltaire

True equality can only mean the
right to be uniquely creative.
—Erik H. Erikson

To blot out of every law book in the land, to sweep
out of every dusty courtroom, to erase from every judge's
mind that centuries-old precedent as to women's inferiori-
ty and dependence and need for protection; to substitute
for it at one blow the simple new precedent of equality,
that is a fight worth making if it takes ten years.
—Crystal Eastman

In America, equality means simply that no handicap
is imposed by society upon any child to prevent
him from realizing the best that is in him.

—*Elliot V. Bell*

Equality is not when a female Einstein gets promoted to
assistant professor: Equality is when a female schlemiel
moves ahead as fast as a male schlemiel.

—*Ewald B. Nyquist*

Accomplishments have no color.

—*Leontyne Price*

Experience, the universal Mother of Sciences.

—*Miguel de Cervantes*

Marriage, to women as to men, must be a luxury,
not a necessity; an incident of life, not all of it. And
the only possible way to accomplish this great change is
to accord to women equal power in the making, shaping
and controlling of the circumstances of life.

—*Susan B. Anthony*

Equality is the result of human
organization. We are not born equal.
—*Hannah Arendt*

Unless man is committed to the belief that all
of amnkind are his brothers, then he labors in vail
and hypocritically in the vineyards of equality.
—*Adam Clayton Powell*

A society that puts equality . . . ahead of freedom
will end up with neither equality nor freedom.
—*Milton and Rose Friedman*

Experience

I have but one lamp by which my feet are guided, and that is the lamp of experience.
— *Patrick Henry*

We learn through experience and experiencing, and no one teaches anyone anything. This is as true for the infant moving from kicking to crawling to walking as it is for the scientist with his equations. If the environment permits it, anyone can learn whatever he chooses to learn; and if the individual permits it, the environment will teach him everything it has to teach.
— *Viola Spolin*

Men are wise in proportion, not to their experience, but to their capacity for experience.
— *George Bernard Shaw*

God will not look you over for medals, degrees, or diplomas, but for scars.
— *Elbert Hubbard*

In my experience, I have always found that you
cannot have an efficient ship unless you have a happy
ship; and you cannot have a happy ship unless you have
an efficient ship. That is the way I intend to start this
commission, and that is the way I intend to go
on—with a happy and efficient ship.
—*Earl Mountbatten of Burma*

Experience is not what happens to you.
It is what you do with what happens to you.
—*Aldous Huxley*

The winds and waves are always
on the side of the ablest navigators.
—*Edward Gibbon*

As experience widens, one begins to see how
much upon a level all human things are.
—*Joseph Farrell*

Nothing is a waste of time if
you use the experience wisely.
—*Auguste Rodin*

Experience is a good teacher, but she sends in terrific bills.
—*Minna Antrim*

Experience: A comb life gives you after you lose your hair.
—*Judith Stern*

You cannot acquire experience by making experiments.
You cannot create experience. You must undergo it.
—*Albert Camus*

Imagination is a poor substitute for experience.
—*Havelock Ellis*

I was thinking that we all learn from experience,
but some of us have to go to summer school.
—*Peter de Vries*

Do not be too timid and squeamish about
your actions. All life is an experience.
—*Ralph Waldo Emerson*

Been there, done that.
—*Michael Caine*

Experience increases our wisdom
but doesn't reduce our follies.
—*Josh Billings*

Experience has no textbooks nor proxies. She demands
that her pupils answer her roll call personally.
—*Minna Antrim*

Measurement of life should be proportioned rather to the
intensity of the experience than to its actual length.
—*Thomas Hardy*

No man's knowledge can go beyond his experience.
—*John Locke*

Experience keeps a dear school,
but fools will learn in no other.
—*Benjamin Franklin*

Faith

Let us have faith that right makes might, and in that faith
let us to the end dare to do our duty as we understand it.

—*Abraham Lincoln*

The smallest seed of faith is better
than the largest fruit of happiness.

—*Henry David Thoreau*

I respect faith, but doubt is what gives you an education.

—*Wilson Mizner*

You don't decide to build a church because you have
money in the bank. You build because God says this
is what I should do. Faith is the supplier of things hoped
for and the evidence of things not seen.

—*Jim Bakker*

Faith is necessary to victory.

—*William Hazlitt*

The beginning of anxiety is the end of faith, and the
beginning of true faith is the end of anxiety.
—*George Mueller*

Nor shall derision prove powerful against those who
listen to humanity or those who follow in the footsteps
of divinity, for they shall live forever. Forever.
—*Kahlil Gibran*

Believe that life is worth living, and
your belief will help create the fact.
—*William James*

Intelligence must follow faith, never
precede it, and never destroy it.
—*Thomas à Kempis*

What I am actually saying is that we need to be
willing to let our intuition guide us, and then be,
willing to follow that guidance directly and fearlessly.
—*Shakti Gawain*

Faith is love taking the form of aspiration.
—*William Ellery Channing*

I claim to be no more than an average man with less than average ability. . . . I have not the shadow of a doubt that any man or woman can achieve what I have, if he or she would make the same effort and cultivate the same hope and faith. Work without faith is like an attempt to reach the bottom of a bottomless pit. . . . My contribution to the great problem lies in my presenting for acceptance truth and ahimsa [nonviolence] in every walk of life, whether for individuals or nations. Nonviolence requires a double faith: Faith in God and also faith in man.

—*Gandhi*

If you can't have faith in what is held up to you for faith, you must find things to believe in yourself, for a life without faith in something is too narrow a space to live.
—*George E. Woodberry*

Only the person who has faith in himself is able to be faithful to others.
—*Erich Fromm*

The first time I shot the hook, I was in fourth
grade, and I was about five feet, eight inches
tall. . . . I was completely confident it would
go in and I've been shooting it ever since.
—*Kareem Abdul-Jabbar*

The only limit to our realization of tomorrow
will be our doubts of today. Let us move
forward with strong and active faith.
—*Franklin D. Roosevelt*

Fate & Destiny

Whatever limits us we call Fate.
—*Ralph Waldo Emerson*

Our destiny changes with our thought; we shall become
what we wish to become, do what we wish to do, when
our habitual thought corresponds with our desire.
—*Orison S. Marden*

Man must understand his universe in
order to understand his destiny.
—*Neil Armstrong*

America lives in the heart of every man
everywhere who wishes to find a region where he
will be free to work out his destiny as he chooses.
—*Woodrow Wilson*

Destiny is what you are supposed to do in life.
Fate is what kicks you in the ass to make you do it.
—*Henry Miller*

Destiny is no matter of chance. It is a matter of choice: It is
not a thing to be waited for, it is a thing to be achieved.
—*William Jennings Bryan*

Man is asked to make of himself what he
is supposed to become to fulfill his destiny.
—*Paul Tillich*

Man's ultimate destiny is to become one
with the Divine Power which governs and
sustains the creation and its creatures.
—*Alfred A. Montapert*

We have no choice of what color we're born
or who our parents are or whether we're rich
or poor. What we do have is some choice over
what we make of our lives once we're here.
—*Mildred D. Taylor*

No trumpets sound when the important decisions
of our life are made. Destiny is made known silently.
—*Agnes de Mille*

Freedom

Freedom is a rare and delicate plant. Our minds tell us,
and history confirms, that the great threat to freedom
is the concentration of power. Government is necessary
to preserve our freedom, it is an instrument through
which we can exercise our freedom; yet by concentrating
power in political hands, it is also a threat to freedom.

—*Milton Friedman*

Freedom is the oxygen of the soul.

—*Moshe Dayan*

America is not a mere body of traders; it is a body
of free men. Our greatness is built upon our freedom—
is moral, not material. We have a great ardor for gain;
but we have a deep passion for the rights of man.

—*Woodrow Wilson*

Without freedom from the past, there is no freedom at all,
because the mind is never new, fresh, innocent.

—*Krishnamurti*

Freedom exists only where the people
take care of the government.
—*Woodrow Wilson*

It is by the goodness of God that in our country
we have those three unspeakably precious things:
freedom of speech, freedom of conscience, and
the prudence never to practice either.
—*Mark Twain*

No man is free who is not a master of himself.
—*Epictetus*

I am certain that, however great the hardships
and the trials which loom ahead, our America will
endure and the cause of human freedom will triumph.
—*Cordell Hull*

Freedom is that instant between when someone tells you
to do something and when you decide how to respond.
—*Jeffrey Borenstein*

Only our individual faith in freedom can keep us free.
—*Dwight D. Eisenhower*

———•———

Freedom is not worth having if it does not
include the freedom to make mistakes.
—*Gandhi*

———•———

People demand freedom of speech as a compensation
for the freedom of thought which they seldom use.
—*Soren Kierkegaard*

———•———

The cost of freedom is always high, but Americans
have always paid it. And one path we shall never choose,
and that is the path of surrender, or submission.
—*John F. Kennedy*

———•———

We look forward to a world founded upon four
essential human freedoms. The first is freedom of
speech and expression. . . . The second is freedom of every
person to worship God in his own way . . . . The third is
freedom from want. . . . The fourth is freedom from fear.
—*Franklin D. Roosevelt*

Once freedom lights its beacon in a man's heart,
the gods are powerless against him.
—*Jean-Paul Satre*

Freedom has its life in the hearts, the actions,
the spirit of men and so it must be daily earned
and refreshed—else like a flower ut from its
life-giving roots, it will wither and die.
—*Dwight D. Eisenhower*

Freedom breeds freedom. Nothing else does
—*Anne Roe*

Freedom prospers when religion is vibrant and
the rule of law under God is acknowledged.
—*Ronald Reagan*

Real freedom is not a matter of the
shifting of advantage from one sex to another.
Real freedom means the disappearance of advantage,
and primarily of economic advantage.
—*Suzanne LaFollette*

There is no freedom on earth orin any star
for those who deny freedom to others.
—*Elbert Hubbard*

Freedom is an internal achievement
rather than an external adjustment
—*Adam Clayton Powell*

Freedom of expression is the matrix, the indispensable
condition, of nearly every other form of freedom.
—*Benjamin Cardozo*

It is not easy to be free men, for to be free you
must afford freedom to your neighbor, regardless
of race, color, creed, or national origin, and that
sometimes, for some is very difficult.
—*Helen Gahagan Douglas*

Be Free, all worthy spirits, And stretch
yourselves, for greatness and for height.
—*George Chapman*

There can be no greater good than the quest for peace,
and no finer purpose than the preservation of freedom.

—*Ronald Reagan*

But what is Freedom? Rightly understood,
A universal license to be good.

—*David Hartley Coleridge*

Freedom means the supremacy
of human rights everywhere.

—*Franklin D. Roosevelt*

Our American values are not luxuries but necessities—
not the salt in our bread but the bread itself. Our
common vision of a free and just society is our greatest
source of cohesion at home and strength abroad—
greater than the bounty of our material blessings.

—*Jimmy Carter*

God wills us free, man wills us slaves,
I will as God wills, God's will be done.

—*Daniel Bliss*

I disapprove of what you say, but I will
defend to the death your right to say it.

—*Voltaire*

The time is now near at hand which must probably
determine whether Americans are to be freemen or slaves;
whether they are to have any property they can call their
own; whether their houses and farms are to be pillaged
and destroyed, and themselves consigned to a state of
wretchedness from which no human efforts will deliver
them. The fate of unborn millions will now depend,
under God, on the courage and conduct of this army.
Our cruel and unrelenting enemy leaves us only the choice
of brave resistance, or the most abject submission. We
have, therefore, to resolve to conquer or die.

—*George Washington*

Freedom belongs to the strong.

—*Richard Wright*

Privacy is absolutely essential to maintaining
a free society. The idea that is at the foundation of the notion of privacy is that the citizen
is not the tool or the instrument of government—
but the reverse. . . . If you have no privacy, it will
tend to follow that you have no political freedom,
no religious freedom, no freedom of families to
make their own decisions. All these freedoms
tend to reinforce one another.

—*Benno C. Schmidt, Jr.*

Fear of serious injury cannot alone jsutify
suppression of free speech and assembly. Men feared
witches and burned women. It is the function of
speech to free men from the bondage of irrational fears.

—*Louis D. Brandeis*

Man is free at the moment he wishes to be.

—*Voltaire*

Friendship

Happy is the house that shelters a friend.
—*Ralph Waldo Emerson*

The only way to have a friend is to be one.
—*Ralph Waldo Emerson*

Each friend represents a world in us, a world
possibly not born until they arrive, and it is only
by this meeting that a new world is born.
—*Anaïs Nin*

I am treating you as my friend asking you
share my present minuses in the hope I can
ask you to share my future pluses.
—*Katherine Mansfield*

If a friend is in trouble, don't annoy him
by asking if there is anything you can do.
Think up something appropriate and do it.
—*Edgar Watson Howe*

Don't bypass the potential for meaningful
friendships just because of differences. Explore
them. Embrace them. Love them.

—*Luci Swindoll*

The real test of friendship is: can you literally
do nothing with the other person? Can you enjoy
those moments of life that are utterly simple?

—*Eugene Kennedy*

Friendship is always a sweet responsibility,
never an opportunity.

—*Kahlil Gibran*

No love, no friendship can cross the path of our
destiny without leaving some mark on it forever.

—*François Marie*

If a man does not make new acquaintances as he advances
through life, he will soon find himself left alone; one
should keep his friendships in constant repair.

—*Samuel Johnson*

Good friends are good for your health.
—*Irwin Sarason*

There is a magnet in your heart that will
attract true friends. That magnet is unselfishness,
thinking of others first . . . when you learn to live
for others, they will live for you.
—*Paramahansa Yogananda*

Friendship without self-interest is one
of the rare and beautiful things of life.
—*James Francis Byrnes*

When my friends lack an eye, I look at them in profile.
—*Joseph Joubert*

Friendship is to feel as one while remaining two.
—*Anne Swetchine*

The language of friendship is not words but meanings.
—*Henry David Thoreau*

It is one of the blessings of old friends that
you can afford to be stupid with them.
—*Ralph Waldo Emerson*

We few, we happy few, we hand of brothers;
For he today that sheds his blood with me
Shall be my brother.
—*William Shakespeare*

Old friends are best. King James used to call
for his old shoes; they were easiest for his feet.
—*John Seldon*

Sometimes our light goes out
but is blown into flame by another human being.
Each of us owes deepest thanks to those
who have rekindled this light.
—*Albert Schweitzer*

We should behave to our friends as we
would wish our friends to behave to us.
—*Aristotle*

True friends stab you in the front.
—*Oscar Wilde*

It is a friendly heart that has plenty of friends.
—*William Thackeray*

Friendship is one of the most tangible things
in a world which offers fewer and fewer supports.
—*Kenneth Branagh*

Be courteous to all, but intimate with few, and
let those few be well tried before you give them
your confidence. True friendship is a plant of slow
growth, and must undergo and withstand the shocks
of adversity before it is entitled to the appellation.
—*George Washington*

Verily great grace may go
With a little gift; and precious are all things that
come from friends.
—*Theocritus*

A friend may well be reckoned
with a masterpiece of nature.
—*George Eliot*

It is easy enough to be friendly to one's friends.
But to befriend your enemy is the quintessence
of true religion. The other is mere business.
—*Gandhi*

The ornament of a house is the friends who frequent it.
—*Ralph Waldo Emerson*

Ah how good it feels! The hand of an old friend!
—*Henry Wadsworth Longfellow*

A friend's writing on an envelope lifts
the heart on the rainiest morning.
—*Charlotte Gray*

One's friends are that part of the human
race with which one can be human.
—*George Santayana*

The finest thing of all about friendship is that
is sends a ray of good hope into the future, and keeps
our hearts from faltering or falling to the wayside.
—*Marcus Tullius Cicero*

When a friend asks there is no tomorrow.
—*George Herbert*

The world is so wide and each of us so
small—yet bound by friendship we are giants.
—*Pam Brown*

True happiness
Consists not in the multitude of friends,
But in the worth and choice.
—*Ben Jonson*

I'm not strong. She's not strong.
But together my friend
and I make the strongest force
in the known universe.
—*Linda MacFarlane*

You cannot be friends upon any other
terms than upon the terms of equality.
—*Woodrow Wilson*

The most beautiful discovery true friends make
is that they can grow separately without growing apart.
—*Elisabeth Foley*

Be a friend to thyself, and others will be so too.
—*Thomas Fuller*

The best mirror is an old friend.
—*George Herbert*

The more we love our friends, the less we flatter them;
it is by excusing nothing that pure love shows itself.
—*Molière*

We secure our friends not by
accepting favors but by doing them.
—*Thucydides*

Friendship with a man is friendship with his virtue,
and does not admit of assumptions of superiority.
—*Mencius*

A friend is, as it were, a second self.
—*Marcus Tullius Cicero*

No man is useless while he has a friend.
—*Robert Louis Stevenson*

The glory of friendship is not the outstretched
hand, nor the kindly smile nor the joy of
companionship; it is the spiritual inspiration that
comes to one when he discovers that someone else
believes in him and is willing to trust him.
—*Ralph Waldo Emerson*

We cannot tell the precise moment when friendship is
formed. As in filling a vessel drop by drop, there is at last a
drop which makes it run over; so in a series of kindnesses
there is at last one which makes the heart run over.
—*James Boswell*

And the song, from beginning to end,
I found again in the heart of a friend.
—*Henry Wadsworth Longfellow*

A friend is someone before whom I may think aloud.
—*Ralph Waldo Emerson*

Without friends no one would choose to live,
though he had all other goods.
—*Aristotle*

Friendship is the hardest thing in the world to explain.
It's not something you learn in school. But if you
haven't learned the meaning of friendship, you
really haven't learned anything.
——*Muhammad Ali*

Friends have all things in common.
—*Plato*

Fun & Play

Ah, why
Should life all labor be?
—*Lord Tennyson*

The mind ought sometimes to be diverted,
that it may return the better to thinking.
—*Phaedrus*

There is a land of pure delight,
Where saints immortal reign;
Infinite day excludes the night,
And pleasures banish pain.
—*Isaac Watts*

The eruption of lived pleasure is such that in losing
myself I find myself; forgetting that I exist, I realize myself.
—*Raoul Vaneigem*

Dost thou think because thou art virtuous,
there shall be no more cakes and ale?
—*William Shakespeare*

Employ thy time well, if thou meanest to gain leisure.
—*Benjamin Franklin*

It is impossible to live pleasurably without
living wisely, well, and justly, and impossible to live
wisely, well and justly without living pleasurably.
—*Epicurus*

If a man insisted always on being serious, and never
allowed himself a bit of fun and relaxation, he would go
mad or become unstable without knowing it.
—*Herodotus*

The secret of happiness is not in doing what
one likes, but in liking what one has to do.
—*James Matthew Barrie*

Choose to have fun. Fun creates enjoyment.
Enjoyment invites participation. Participation
focuses attention. Attention expands awareness.
Awareness promotes insight. Insight generates knowledge.
Knowledge facilitates action. Action yields results.
—*Oswald B. Shallow*

If we bring a little joy into your humdrum lives, it makes us feel our work ain't been in vain for nothin'.
—*Jean Hagen in* Singin' in the Rain

I think the only reason you should retire is if you can find something you enjoy doing more than what you're doing now. I happen to be in love with show business, and I can't think of anything I'd enjoy more than that. So I guess I've been retired all my life.
—*George Burns*

Variety is the soul of pleasure.
—*Aphra Behn*

What makes men happy is liking what they have to do. This is a principle on which society is not founded.
—*Claude Adrien Helvetius*

He who binds to himself a job
Does the winged life destroy;
But he who kisses the joy as it flies
Lives in eternity's sunrise.
—*William Blake*

By happy alchemy of mind
They turn to pleasure all they find.
—*Matthew Green*

Rich the treasure,
Sweet the pleasure—
Sweet is pleasure after pain.
—*John Dryden*

The secret of a happy life is to delight in duty. When duty becomes delight, then burdens become blessings.
—*Warren Wiersbe*

The Future

The strongest and sweetest songs yet remain to be sung.
—Walt Whitman

In the future everyone will be
world-famous for fifteen minutes.
—Andy Warhol

The world is full of people whose notion of a satisfactory
future is, in fact, a return to the idealized past.
—Robertson Davies

The best way to secure future happiness is
to be as happy as is rightfully possible today.
—Charles W. Eliot

Tomorrow is the most important thing in life.
Comes in to us at midnight very clean. It's perfect
when it arrives and it pours itself in our hands and
hopes we've learnt something from yesterday.
—John Wayne

It is the past, not the dizzy present,
that is the best door to the future.
—*Camille Paglia*

Twenty years from now you will be more
disappointed by the things that you didn't do than
by the ones you did do. So throw off the bowlines.
Sail away from the safe harbor. Catch the trade winds
in your sails. Explore. Dream. Discover.
—*Mark Twain*

The future comes one day at a time.
—*Dean Acheson*

I hold that man is in the right who
is most closely in league with the future.
—*Henrik Ibsen*

Never let the future disturb you. You will meet
it, if you have to, with the same weapons of reason
which today arm you against the present.
—*Marcus Aurelius Antoninus*

It is never safe to look into the future with eyes of fear.
—*Edward H. Harriman*

The farther back you can look,
the farther forward you are likely to see.
—*Winston Churchill*

Our country is still young and its potential is still enormous. We should remember, as we look toward the future, that the more fully we believe in and achieve freedom and equal opportunity—not simply for ourselves but for others—the greater our accomplishments as a nation will be.
—*Henry Ford II*

Every age needs men who will redeem the
time by living with a vision of things that are to be.
—*Adlai Stevenson*

The future belongs to us. In order to
do great things one must be enthusiastic.
—*Comte Henri de Saint-Simon*

You are today where your thoughts have brought you;
you will be tomorrow where your thoughts take you.
—*James Allen*

It is a mistake to look too far ahead. Only one
link in the chain of destiny can be handled at a time.
—*Winston Churchill*

I like the dreams of the future
better than the history of the past.
—*Patrick Henry*

My interest is in the future because I am
going to spend the rest of my life there.
—*Charles F. Kettering*

Light tomorrow with today!
—*Elizabeth Barrett Browning*

The future is not a gift—it is an achievement.
—*Harry Lauder*

Genius

To believe your own thought, to believe that
what is true for you in your private heart is
true for all men—that is genius.
—*Ralph Waldo Emerson*

Men of genius do not excel in any profession because
they labor in it, but they labor in it because they excel.
—*William Hazlitt*

Genius without education is like silver in the mine.
—*Benjamin Franklin*

Improvement makes straight roads; but the crooked
roads without improvement are roads of genius.
—*William Blake*

The kind of intelligence a genius has is a different
sort of intelligence. The thinking of a genius does not
proceed logically. It leaps with great ellipses. It pulls
knowledge from God knows where.
—*Dorothy Thompson*

Any intelligent fool can make things bigger, more complex, and more violent. It takes a touch of genius— and a lot of courage—to move in the opposite direction.
—*Albert Einstein*

Genius is the ability to act wisely without precedent —the power to do the right thing the first time.
—*Elbert Hubbard*

Genius seems to be the faculty of having faith in everything, and especially oneself.
—*Arthur Stringer*

When Nature has work to be done, she creates a genius to do it.
—*Ralph Waldo Emerson*

Genius develops in quiet places, character out in the full current of human life.
—*Johann Wolfgang von Goethe*

When human power becomes so great and
original that we can account for it only as a kind
of divine imagination, we call it genius.
—*William Crashaw*

—•—

Genius is an infinite capacity for taking pains.
—*Thomas Carlyle*

—•—

Common sense is instinct, and enough of it is genius.
—*Josh Billings*

—•—

To know one's self is wisdom, but
to know one's neighbor is genius.
—*Minna Antrim*

—•—

Genius is entitled to respect only when it promotes
the peace and improves the happiness of mankind.
—*Lord Essex*

—•—

Talent is that which is in a man's power;
genius is that in whose power a man is.
—*James Russell Lowell*

Doing easily what others find difficult is talent;
doing what is impossible for talent is genius.
—*Henri Frédéric Amiel*

Genius is no snob. It does not run after titles
or seek by preference the high circles of society.
—*Woodrow Wilson*

Geniuses are the luckiest of mortals because what they
must do is the same as what they most want to do.
—*W. H. Auden*

Genius . . . is the capacity to see ten things where
the ordinary man sees one, and where the man of
talent sees two or three, plus the ability to register
that multiple perception in the material of his art.
—*Ezra Pound*

Giving, Service & Charity

The human contribution is the essential ingredient. It is only in the giving of oneself to others that we truly live.
—*Ethel Percy Andrus*

Generosity is giving more than you can,
and pride is taking less than you need.
—*Kahlil Gibran*

It is one of the beautiful compensations of
this life that no one can sincerely try to help
another without helping himself.
—*Charles Dudley Warner*

Out of the best and most productive years of each
man's life, he should carve a segment in which he puts
his private career aside to serve his community and his
country, and thereby serve his children, his neighbours,
his fellow men, and the cause of freedom.
—*David Lilienthal*

Many men have been capable of doing a wise thing, more a cunning thing, but very few a generous thing.

—*Alexander Pope*

For anything worth having one must pay the price; and the price is always work, patience, love, self-sacrifice—no paper currency, no promises to pay, but the gold of real service.

—*John Burroughs*

Service is the rent we pay for being.
It is the very purpose of life,
and not something you do in your spare time.

—*Marion Wright Edelman*

Almsgiving tends to perpetuate poverty; aid does away with it once and for all. Almsgiving leaves a man just where he was before. Aid restores him to society as an individual worthy of all respect and not as a man with a grievance. Almsgiving is the generosity of the rich; social aid levels up social inequalities. Charity separates the rich from the poor; aid raises the needy and sets him on the same level with the rich.

—*Eva Perón*

Self-sacrifice is the real miracle out of
which all the reported miracles grow.
—*Ralph Waldo Emerson*

You give but little when you give of your possessions.
It is when you give of yourself that you truly give.
—*Kahlil Gibran*

If there be any truer measure of a man than
by what he does, it must be by what he gives.
—*Robert South*

We tire of those pleasures we take,
but never of those we give.
—*John Petit-Senn*

Everybody can be great . . . because anybody can serve. You
don't have to have a college degree to serve. You don't have
to make your subject and verb agree to serve. You only
need a heart full of grace. A soul generated by love.
—*Martin Luther King, Jr.*

To those people in the huts and villages of half the globe struggling to break the bonds of mass misery, we pledge our best efforts to help them help themselves, for whatever period is required, not because the Communists may be doing it, not because we seek their votes, but because it is right. If a free society cannot help the many who are poor, it cannot save the few who are rich.

—John F. Kennedy

Every charitable act is a stepping-stone toward heaven.

—Henry Ward Beecher

Those who bring sunshine to the lives of others cannot keep it from themselves.

—James Matthew Barrie

Only a life lived for others is the life worthwhile.

—Albert Einstein

The more one loves, the stronger becomes the capacity for loving, and it is the hands that are always busy with helpfulness that always find yet more to do.

—Maud Ballington Booth

The first great gift we can bestow
on others is a good example.

—*Thomas Morell*

———•———

Give to him who asks of you, and do not turn
away from him who wants to borrow from you.

—*adapted from Matthew 5:42*

———•———

No man is born unto himself alone;
Who lives unto himself, he lives to none.

—*Francis Quarles*

———•———

From what we get, we can make a living;
what we give, however, makes a life.

—*Arthur Ashe*

———•———

The only gift is a portion of thyself.

—*Ralph Waldo Emerson*

———•———

Real unselfishness consists in
sharing the interests of others.

—*George Santayana*

181

When we frankly give, forever is our own.
—*George Granville*

It is more blessed to give than to receive.
—*adapted from Acts 20:35*

Teach us to give and not to count the cost.
—*Ignatius Loyola*

I hate the giving of the hand unles
the whole man accompanies it.
—*Ralph Waldo Emerson*

The manner of giving is worth more than the gift.
—*Pierre Corneille*

A successful man is he who receives a great
deal from his fellow men, usually incomparably
more than corresponds to his service to them. The
value of a man, however, should be seen in what he
gives and not in what he is able to receive.
—*Albert Einstein*

Giving is the highest expression of potency.

—*Enrich Fromm*

In charity there is no excess.

—*Francis Bacon*

Sometimes give your services for nothing, calling to mind a precious benefaction or present satisfaction. And if there be an opportunity of serving one who is a stranger in financial straits, give full assistance to all such. For where this is love of man, there is also love of the art.

—*Hippocrates*

Real giving had its joy in imagining the joy of the receiver. It means choosing, expending time, going out of one's way, thinking of the other as a subject: the opposite of distraction.

—*Theodor W. Adorno*

When you cease to make a contribution you begin to die.

—*Eleanor Roosevelt*

If you find it in your heart to care for
somebody else, you will have succeeded.
—*Maya Angelou*

No man has a right to lead such a life of contemplation as
to forget in his own ease the service due to his neighbor.
—*St. Augustine*

The meaning of good and bad, of better
and worse, is simply helping or hurting.
—*Ralph Waldo Emerson*

Each time anyone comes into contact with us,
they must become different and better people
because of having met us.
We must radiate God's love.
We must know that we have been created for greater things,
not just to be a number in the world,
not just to go for diplomas and degrees,
this work and that work.
We have been created in order to love and to be loved.
Love does not measure . . . it just gives.
—*Mother Teresa*

Goals & Direction

Aim at perfection in everything, though in most things it is
unattainable. However, they who aim at it, and persevere,
will come much nearer to it than those whose laziness and
despondency make them give it up as unattainable.

—*Lord Chesterfield*

The significance of a man is not in what he
attains but rather in what he longs to attain.

—*Kahlil Gibran*

It is reasonable to have perfection in our eye that
we may always advance toward it, though we
know it can never be reached.

—*Samuel Johnson*

Winning isn't everything, but wanting to win is.

—*Vince Lombardi*

Don't bother just to be better than your contemporaries
or predecessors. Try to be better than yourself.

—*William Faulkner*

Existence is a strange bargain. Life owes us little;
we owe it everything. The only true happiness
comes from squandering ourselves for a purpose.
—*William Cowper*

Not to enjoy life, but to employ life,
ought to be our aim and inspiration.
—*John Ross MacDuff*

Aim at the sun, and you may not reach it;
but your arrow will fly far higher than if
aimed at an object on a level with yourself.
—*Joel Hawes*

The crowning fortune of a man is to be born
to some pursuit which finds him employment and
happiness, whether it be to make baskets, or
broadswords, or canals, or statues, or songs.
—*Ralph Waldo Emerson*

Give me but one firm spot on which
to stand, and I will move the earth.
—*Archimedes*

Not failure, but low aim, is crime.
>—*James Russell Lowell*

Go for the moon. If you don't get it,
you'll still be heading for a star.
>—*Willis Reed*

Jesus spoke to them, saying, 'I am the light of the
world; he who follows Me shall not walk in the
darkness, but shall have the light of life.'
>—*adapted from John 8:12*

If you wish to reach the highest, begin at the lowest.
>—*Publilius Syrus*

Striving for excellence motivates you;
striving for perfection is demoralizing.
>—*Harriet Braiker*

Those who aim at great deeds must also suffer greatly.
>—*Marcus Licinius Crassus*

187

Great minds have purposes, others have wishes.
—*Washington Irving*

High aims form high character, and
great objects bring out great minds.
—*Tryon Edwards*

When you are aspiring to the highest place, it is
honorable to reach the second or even the third rank.
—*Marcus Tullius Cicero*

We aim above the mark to hit the mark.
—*Ralph Waldo Emerson*

Nothing contributes so much to tranquilize the
mind as a steady purpose—a point on which
the soul may fix its intellectual eye.
—*Mary Wollstonecraft Shelley*

In the long run men hit only what they aim at.
—*Henry David Thoreau*

Harmony of aim, not identity of
conclusion, is the secret of sympathetic life.
—*Ralph Waldo Emerson*

When you reach for the stars, you may not quite get one,
but you won't come up with a handful of mud either.
—*Leo Burnett*

I find the great thing in this world is not so much
where we stand, as in what direction we are moving:
To reach the port of heaven, we must sail sometimes
with the wind and sometimes against it—but we must
sail, and not drift, nor lie at anchor.
—*Oliver Wendell Holmes*

If a man aspires to the highest place, it is no dishonor
to him to halt at the second, or even at the third.
—*Marcus Tullius Cicero*

Who strives always to the utmost,
For him there is salvation.
—*Johann Wolfgang von Goethe*

There are two things to aim at in life: first, to
get what you want, and after that to enjoy it.
—*Logan Pearsall Smith*

There are no rules around here! We
are trying to accomplish something!
—*Thomas Edison*

The pursuit of perfection, then, is the pursuit of
sweetness and light. He who works for sweetness and
light, works to make reason and the will of God prevail.
—*Matthew Arnold*

It seems to me we can never give up longing and
wishing while we are thoroughly alive. There are
certain things we feel to be beautiful and good
and we must hunger after them.
—*George Eliot*

The world stands aside to let anyone
pass who knows where he is going.
—*David Starr Jordan*

At any given moment life is completely
senseless. But viewed over a period, it seems to
reveal itself as an organism existing in time, having
a purpose, tending in a certain direction.

—*Aldous Huxley*

Ideals are like stars; you will not succeed in touching
them with your hands, but like the seafaring man
on the desert of waters, you choose them as your guides,
and following them, you reach your destiny.

—*Carl Schurz*

The most absurd and reckless aspirations
have sometimes led to extraordinary success.

—*Luc de Clapiers*

Love our principle, order our
foundation, progress our goal.

—*Auguste Comte*

If you would hit the mark, you must aim a little above it:
Every arrow that flies feels the attraction of earth.

—*Henry Wadsworth Longfellow*

191

I long to accomplish a great and noble task, but
it is my chief duty to accomplish small tasks
as if they were great and noble.
—*Helen Keller*

A successful individual typically sets his next goal
somewhat but not too much above his last achievement.
In this way he steadily raises his level of aspiration.
—*Kurt Lewin*

A winner is someone who recognizes his God-given
talents, works his tail off to develop them into skills,
and uses these skills to accomplish his goals.
—*Larry Bird*

God & Angels

Love not Pleasure; love God.
—*Thomas Carlyle*

The soul of God is poured into the
world through the thoughts of men.
—*Ralph Waldo Emerson*

The universe is one of God's thoughts.
—*Johann von Schiller*

God's providence is on the side of clear heads.
—*Henry Ward Beecher*

Perfection consists not in doing extraordinary things,
but in doing ordinary things extraordinarily well. Neglect
nothing; the most trivial action may be performed to God.
—*Angelique Arnauld*

Because God's gifts put man's best dreams to shame.
—*Elizabeth Barrett Browning*

A man with God is always in the majority.
—*John Knox*

The mind of a man plans his way,
But the Lord directs his steps.
—*adapted from Proverbs 16:9*

Now, God be prais'd, that to believing souls
Gives light in darkness, comfort in despair!
—*William Shakespeare*

Prayer is our pathway not only to divine protection,
but also to a personal, intimate relationship to God.
—*Shirley Dobson*

Let nothing disturb thee,
Let nothing affright thee,
All passeth away,
God alone will stay,
Patience obtaineth all things.
Who God possesseth, is lacking in nothing
God alone sufficeth.
—*Saint Teresa of Avila*

Whatever God's dream about man may be, it seems
certain it cannot come true unless man cooperates.
—*Stella Terrill Mann*

Whoever obeys the gods, to him they particularly listen.
—*Homer*

If God did not exist, it would be necessary to invent him.
—*Voltaire*

You shall have joy, or you shall have power,
said God; you shall not have both.
—*Ralph Waldo Emerson*

One on God's side is a majority.
—*Wendell Phillips*

Two men please God—who serves Him with all
his heart because he knows Him; who seeks Him
with all his heart because he knows Him not.
—*Nikita Ivanovich Panin*

It is the quality of our work which will
please God and not the quantity.

—Gandhi

Life is everything. Life is God. Everything changes and
moves and that movement is God. And while there is life
there is joy in consciousness of the divine. To love life is to
love God. Harder and more blessed than all else is to love
this life in one's sufferings, in innocent sufferings.

—Leo Tolstoy

If I take the wings of the dawn,
If I dwell in the remotest part of the sea,
Even there Thy hand will lay hold of me.

—adapted from Psalms 139:9–10

Self-reliance, the height and perfection
of man, is reliance on God.

—Ralph Waldo Emerson

The fewer our wants, the nearer we resemble the gods.

—Socrates

The longer I live, the more convincing proofs I see of
this truth, that God governs in the affairs of man; and if
a sparrow cannot fall to the ground without his notice, is
it probable that an empire can rise without his aid?
—*Benjamin Franklin*

Often God has to shut a door in our face,
so that He can subsequently open the door
through which He wants us to go.
—*Catherine Marshall*

An act of God was defined as something
which no reasonable man could have expected.
—*A. P. Herbert*

Man may dismiss compassion from
his heart, but God never will.
—*William Cowper*

When God crowns our merits, he is
crowning nothing other than his gifts.
—*St. Augustine*

The glory of God is in man fully alive.
—*St. Irenaeus*

The best way to know God is to love many things.
—*Vincent van Gogh*

The angels keep their ancient places;
Turn but a stone and start a wing!
'Tis ye, 'tis your estranged faces,
That miss the many-splendoured thing.
—*Francis Thompson*

God enters by a private door into every individual.
—*Ralph Waldo Emerson*

Try thyself first, and after call in God. For
to the worker God himself lends aid.
—*Euripides*

Even God lends a hand to honest boldness.
—*Menander*

Men talk of "Finding God," but no wonder it is
difficult; He is hidden in that darkest hiding-place,
your heart. You yourself are a part of Him.

—*Christopher Morley*

Even a god cannot change the past.

—*Agathon*

In the faces of men and women I see God.

—*Walt Whitman*

Through all Eternity to Thee
A joyful Song I'll raise,
For oh! Eternity's too short
To utter all thy Praise.

—*Joseph Addison*

He who created you without you
will not justify you without you.

—*St. Augustine*

In Reason's ear they all rejoice,
And utter forth a glorious voice,
For ever singing, as they shine:
The hand that made us is divine.

—*Joseph Addison*

Were I a nightingale, I would sing like a nightingale;
were I a swan, like a swan. But as it is, I am a rational
being, therefore I must sing hymns of praise to God.

—*Epictetus*

And all must love the human form
In heathen, turk, or jew;
Where Mercy, Love & Pity dwell
There God is dwelling too.

—*William Blake*

The rich man in his castle,
The poor man at his gate,
God made them, high or lowly,
And ordered their estate.

—*Cecil Frances Alexander*

Heartily know,
When half-gods go,
The gods arrive.
—*Ralph Waldo Emerson*

Get ready for God to show you not only
His pleasure, but His approval.
—*Joni Eareckson Tada*

We are in God's hand.
—*William Shakespeare*

Your talent is God's gift to you.
What you do with it is your gift back to God.
—*Leo Buscaglia*

God tempers the wind, said Maria, to the shorn lamb.
—*Laurence Sterne*

God is the brave man's hope, and not the coward's excuse.
—*Plutarch*

Live with the gods.
—*Marcus Aurelius Antoninus*

God has given each normal person a capacity to
achieve some end. True, some are endowed with more
talent than others, but God has left none of us untalented.
—*Martin Luther King, Jr.*

Prayer indeed is good, but while calling
on the gods a man should himself lend a hand.
—*Hippocrates*

There is no pit so deep that God's love is not deeper still.
—*Corrie ten Boom*

Cast all your cares on God; that anchor holds.
—*Lord Tennyson*

All men have need of the gods.

—*Homer*

Greatness

Greatness is a zigzag streak of lightning in the brain.
>—*Herbert Asquith*

Lives of great men all remind us
We can make our lives sublime.
And, departing, leave behind us
Footprints on the sands of time.
>—*Henry Wadsworth Longfellow*

Nothing is more simple than greatness;
indeed, to be simple is to be great.
>—*Ralph Waldo Emerson*

How glorious it is, but how painful it is also,
to be exceptional in this world.
>—*Alfred de Musset*

You stand in your own light.
>—*John Heywood*

I too shall lie in the dust when I am dead,
but now let me win noble renown.

—*Homer*

The real difference between men is energy. A strong
will, a settled purpose, and invincible determination,
can accomplish almost anything; and in this lies the
distinction between great men and little men.

—*Thomas Fuller*

Greatness, generally speaking, is an unusual quantity
of a usual quality grafted upon a common man.

—*William Allen White*

To endure is greater than to dare; to tire out
hostile fortune; to be daunted by no difficulty; to
keep heart when all have lost it; to go through intrigue
spotless; to forgo even ambition when the end is gained—
who can say this is not greatness?

—*William Makepeace Thackeray*

What is excellent becomes the permanent.

—*Jane Addams*

Responsibility is the price of greatness.
—*Winston Churchill*

It is an easy matter, requiring little thought, generosity or statesmanship to push a weak man down when he is struggling to get up. Anyone can do that. Greatness, generosity, statesmanship are shown in stimulating, encouraging every individual in the body politic to make of himself the most useful, intelligent and patriotic citizen possible.
—*Booker T. Washington*

The superior man will not manifest either narrow-mindedness or the want of self-respect.
—*Mencius*

Great men are they who see that spiritual is stronger than any material force, that thoughts rule the world.
—*Ralph Waldo Emerson*

To be a great man and a saint for oneself, that is the one important thing.
—*Charles Baudelaire*

205

Shakespeare was the great one before us.
His place was between God and despair.
—*Eugène Ionesco*

Behind almost every great man there stands
either a good parent or a good teacher.
—*Gilbert Highet*

Little minds are interested in the extraordinary;
great minds in the commonplace.
—*Elbert Hubbard*

It is not the strength, but the duration,
of great sentiments that makes great men.
—*Friedrich Nietzsche*

You cannot fly like an eagle with the wings of a wren.
—*William Henry Hudson*

Nothing great was ever achieved without enthusiasm.
—*Ralph Waldo Emerson*

High station in life is earned by the gallantry with
which appalling experiences are survived with grace.
—*Tennessee Williams*

Greatness is a road leading towards the unknown.
—*Charles de Gaulle*

Great men hallow a whole people,
and lift up all who live in their time.
—*Sydney Smith of Macaulay*

The world knows nothing of its greatest men.
—*Henry Taylor*

And there is no greatness where there
is not simplicity, goodness, and truth.
—*Leo Tolstoy*

The ideal condition
Would be, I admit, that men should be right by instinct;
Man is the measure of all things.
—Protagoras

Great thoughts come from the heart.
—Luc de Clapiers

It is natural to believe in great men. If the companions
of our childhood should turn out to be heroes, and
their condition regal it would not surprise us. All
mythology opens with demigods, and the circumstance
high and poetic; that is, their genius is paramount.
—Ralph Waldo Emerson

Numberless are the world's wonders, but none
More wonderful than man.
—Sophocles

It is a rough road that leads to the heights of greatness.
—Lucius Annaeus Seneca

Happiness

Happiness makes up for in height what it lacks in length.
—*Robert Frost*

The good life, as I conceive it, is a happy life.
I do not mean that if you are good you will be happy—
I mean that if you are happy you will be good.
—*Bertrand Russell*

Even if happiness forgets you a little bit,
never completely forget about it.
—*Jacques Prévert*

The greatest happiness for the thinking man
is to have fathomed the fathomable, and to
quietly revere the unfathomable.
—*Johann Wolfgang von Goethe*

Man's real life is happy, chiefly because he
is ever expecting that it soon will be so.
—*Edgar Allan Poe*

But what is happiness except the simple
harmony between a man and the life he leads?

—*Albert Camus*

Follow your bliss.

—*Joseph Campbell*

We learn the inner secret of happiness when
we learn to direct our inner drives, our interest
and attention to something outside ourselves.

—*Ethel Percy Andrus*

Happiness comes of the capacity to feel deeply, to
enjoy simply, to think freely, to risk life, to be needed.

—*Storm Jameson*

Too much of a good thing can be wonderful.

—*Mae West*

Anything you're good at contributes to happiness.

—*Bertrand Russell*

There is only one happiness in life,
to love and be loved.
—*George Sand*

To fill the hour—that is happiness.
—*Ralph Waldo Emerson*

Joy is not in things; it is in us.
—*Richard Wagner*

Happiness? That's nothing more
than health and a poor memory.
—*Albert Schweitzer*

Happiness is the way-station
between two little and too much.
—*Channing Pollock*

Learning to live in the present
moment is part of the path of joy
—*Sarah Ban Breathnach*

May we never let the things we can't have, or
don't have, or shouldn't have, spoil our enjoyment
of the things we do have and can have. As we value
our happiness let us not forget it, for one of the
greatest lessons in life is learning to be happy without
the things we cannot or should not have.

—*Richard L. Evans*

Happiness is a warm puppy.

—*Charles M. Schulz*

The grand essentials of happiness are: something to do,
something to love, and something to hope for.

—*Allan K. Chalmers*

Morality is not properly the doctrine of how
we may make ourselves happy, but how we may
make ourselves worthy of happiness.

—*Immanuel Kant*

Thus happiness depends, as Nature shows,
Less on exterior things than most suppose.

—*William Cowper*

That is happiness; to be dissolved
into something complete and great.
—*Willa Cather*

If you are content, you have enough to live comfortably.
—*Titus Maccius Plautus*

Happiness isn't something you
experience; it's something you remember.
—*Oscar Levant*

"What would you call the highest happiness?"
Wratislaw was asked. "The sense of competence,"
was the answer, given without hesitation.
—*John Buchan*

One should not seek happiness, but rather happy people.
—*Coco Chanel*

Resolve to be thyself: and know, that he
Who finds himself, loses his misery.
—*Matthew Arnold*

Happiness is the highest good, being a realization
and perfect practice of virtue, which some can attain,
while others have little or none of it . . .

—*Aristotle*

We must select the illusion which appeals to our temperament, and embrace it with passion, if we want to be happy.

—*Cyril Connolly*

There is only one way to happiness and
that is to cease worrying about things which
are beyond the power of our will.

—*Epictetus*

Many persons have a wrong idea of what constitutes
true happiness. It is not attained through self-gratification
but through fidelity to a worthy purpose.

—*Helen Keller*

Human felicity is produced not so much by
great pieces of good fortune that seldom happen,
as by little advantages that occur every day.

—*Benjamin Franklin*

My creed is that:
Happiness is the only good.
The place to be happy is here.
The time to be happy is now.
The way to be happy is to make others so.
—*Robert G. Ingersoll*

Winning is important to me, but what
brings me real joy is the experience of being
fully engaged in whatever I'm doing.
—*Phil Jackson*

The will of man is his happiness.
—*Friedrich von Schiller*

The human spirit needs to accomplish,
to achieve, to triumph, to be happy.
—*Ben Stein*

Thousands of candles can be lighted from a single
candle, and the life of the candle will not be shortened.
Happiness never decreases by being shared.
—*Buddha*

Happiness is the light on the water.
The water is cold and dark and deep.
—*William Maxwell*

———

To be happy, we must not be too concerned with others.
—*Albert Camus*

———

My life has no purpose, no direction, no aim,
no meaning, and yet I'm happy. I can't figure it out.
What am I doing right?
—*Charles M. Schulz*

———

All who joy would win must share it.
Happiness was born a twin.
—*Lord Byron*

———

Pleasure is the beginning and the end of living happily.
—*Epicurus*

———

Happiness and peace are found when we are in harmony
with ourselves, with God, and with our fellowmen.
—*Barbara W. Winder*

Men's happiness springs mainly from
moderate troubles, which afford the mind a
healthful stimulus, and are followed by a reaction
which produces a cheerful flow of spirits.
—*Edward Wigglesworth*

There is no duty we so much
underrate as the duty of being happy.
—*Robert Louis Stevenson*

The formula for complete happiness is
to be very busy with the unimportant.
—*A. Edward Newton*

Happiness is a mystery like religion,
and it should never be rationalized.
—*G. K. Chesterton*

The secret of contentment is knowing how
to enjoy what you have, and to be able to lose
all desire for things beyond your reach.
—*Lin Yutang*

It has never been given to a man to
attain at once his happiness and his salvation.
—*Charles Peguy*

Your success and happiness lie in you. . . . Resolve
to keep happy, and your joy and you shall form
an invincible host against difficulties.
—*Helen Keller*

If thou workest at that which is before thee, following
right reason seriously, vigorously, calmly, without allowing
anything else to distress thee, but keeping thy divine part
pure, as if thou shouldst be bound to give it back immediately; if thou holdest to this, expecting nothing, fearing
nothing, but satisfied with the present activity according to
Nature, and with heroic truth in every word and sound
which thou utterest, thou wilt live happy. And there is no
man who is able to prevent this.
—*Marcus Aurelius Antoninus*

Man needs, for his happiness, not only the enjoyment
of this or that, but hope and enterprise and change.
—*Bertrand Russell*

Heroism

Heroism feels and never reasons
and therefore is always right.
—*Ralph Waldo Emerson*

If a man hasn't discovered something
that he will die for, he isn't fit to live.
—*Martin Luther King, Jr.*

In our world of big names, curiously, our true heroes
tend to be anonymous. In this life of illusion and quasi-
illusion, the person of solid virtues who can be admired
for something more substantial than his well-knownness
often proves to be the unsung hero: the teacher, the nurse,
the mother, the honest cop, the hard worker at lonely,
underpaid, unglamorous, unpublicized jobs.
—*Daniel J. Boorstin*

To stand upon the ramparts and die for our
principles is heroic, but to sally forth to battle and
win for our principles is something more than heroic.
—*Franklin D. Roosevelt*

Self-trust is the essence of heroism.
—*Ralph Waldo Emerson*

Claret is the liquor for boys; port for men; but
he who aspires to be a hero must drink brandy.
—*Samuel Johnson*

I think of a hero as someone who understands the
degree of responsibility that comes with his freedom.
—*Bob Dylan*

The ordinary man is involved in action,
the hero acts. An immense difference.
—*Henry Miller*

The world's battlefields have been in the heart
chiefly; more heroism has been displayed in the
household and in the closet, than on the most
memorable battlefields in history.
—*Henry Ward Beecher*

Most people aren't appreciated enough, and the bravest things we do in our lives are usually known only to ourselves. No one throws ticker tape on the man who chose to be faithful to his wife, on the lawyer who didn't take the drug money, or the daughter who held her tongue again and again. All this anonymous heroism.

—*Peggy Noonan*

One of the forms of psychological heroism is the willingness to tolerate anxiety and uncertainty in the pursuit of our values—whether these values be work goals, the love of another human being, the raising of a family or personal growth.

—*Samuel Branden*

Nurture your mind with great thoughts;
to believe in the heroic makes heroes.

—*Benjamin Disraeli*

See, the conquering hero comes!
Sound the trumpet, beat the drums!

—*Thomas Morell*

A hero is no braver than an ordinary man,
but he is brave five minutes longer.
—*Ralph Waldo Emerson*

The opportunities for heroism are limited in this kind of world: the most people can do is sometimes not to be as weak as they've been at other times.
—*Angus Wilson*

It's true that heroes are inspiring, but mustn't they also do some rescuing if they are to be worthy of their name? Would Wonder Woman matter if she only sent commiserating telegrams to the distressed?
—*Jeannette Winterson*

Hopes & Dreams

A man's dreams are an index to his greatness.

—Zadok Rabinwitz

Hope is the thing with feathers,
That perches in the soul,
And sings the tune—without the words,
And never stops—at all. . .

—Emily Dickinson

A man's gotta dream; it comes with the territory.

—Fredric March

Cherish your visions and your dreams as they
are the children of your soul; the blue prints
of your ultimate achievements.

—Napoleon Hill

Keep true to the dreams of thy youth.

—Johann von Schiller

One of the most adventurous things left us is to
go to bed. For no one can lay a hand on our dreams.
—*E. V. Lucas*

Dreams are the touchstones of our character.
—*Henry David Thoreau*

All men who have achieved great
things have been great dreamers.
—*Orison S. Marden*

Throw your dreams into space like a kite,
and you do not know what it will bring back,
a new life, a new friend, a new love, a new country.
—*Anaïs Nin*

The future belongs to those who
believe in the beauty of their dreams.
—*Eleanor Roosevelt*

While there's life, there's hope.
—*Terence*

Reality is wrong. Dreams are for real.
—*Tupac Shakur*

The smaller the head, the bigger the dream.
—*Austin O'Malley*

Hope is a state of mind, not of the world. Hope,
in this deep and powerful sense, is not the same as joy
that things are going well, or willingness to invest in
enterprises that are obviously heading for success, but
rather an ability to work for something because it is good.
—*Václav Havel*

America is too great for small dreams.
—*Ronald Reagan*

When I was a beggarly boy,
And lived in a cellar damp,
I had not a friend nor a toy,
But I had Alladin's lamp.
—*James Russell Lowell*

Dreaming is an act of pure imagination, attesting in
all men a creative power, which, if it were available in
waking, would make every man a Dante or Shakespeare.
—*H. F. Hedge*

Whatever you can do or dream you can, begin it.
Boldness has genius, power, and magic in it. Begin it now.
—*Johann Wolfgang von Goethe*

If one advances confidently in the direction of his dreams,
and endeavors to live the life which he has imagined, he
will meet with a success unexpected in common hours.
—*Henry David Thoreau*

Reverie is not a mind vacuum. It is rather the gift of an
hour which knows the plentitude of the soul.
—*Gaston Bachelard*

Dreams come true; without that possibility,
nature would not incite us to have them.
—*John Updike*

You see things; and you say "Why?"; But I dream
things that never were; and I say "Why not?"
—*George Bernard Shaw*

The spirit within you remains a free thing
filled with boundless dreams to share.
—*Flavia*

We have always held to the hope, the belief,
the conviction, that there is a better life, a
better world, beyond the horizon.
—*Franklin D. Roosevelt*

All men of action are dreamers.
—*James G. Huneker*

Dreams are renewable. No matter what our age
or condition, there are still untapped possibilities
within us and new beauty waiting to be born.
—*Dale E. Turner*

It is difficult to say what is impossible, for the dream of yesterday is the hope of today and the reality of tomorrow.

—*Robert H. Goddard*

Hope, like faith, is nothing if it is not courageous;
it is nothing if it is not ridiculous.

—*Thornton Wilder*

We are near awakening when we dream that we dream.

—*Novalis*

There will always be dreams grander or humbler
than your own, but there will never be a dream
exactly like your own . . . for you are unique and
more wondrous than you know!

—*Linda Staten*

Nothing that is worth anything can be achieved in a
lifetime; therefore we must be saved by hope.

—*Reinhold Niebuhr*

We grow great by dreams. All big men are dreamers. They see things in the soft haze of a spring day or in the red fire of a long winter's evening. Some of us let these great dreams die, but others nourish and protect them; nurse them through bad days till they bring them to the sunshine and light which comes always to those who sincerely hope that their dreams will come true.

—*Woodrow Wilson*

I think the truly natural things are dreams,
   which nature can't touch with decay.

—*Bob Dylan*

I love those who yearn for the impossible.

—*Johann Wolfgang von Goethe*

Without hope we live in desire.

—*Dante Alighieri*

Fear cannot be without hope nor hope without fear.

—*Benedict Spinoza*

If you can dream it, you can do it.
—*Walt Disney*

In all things it is better to hope than to despair.
—*Johann Wolfgang von Goethe*

If one advances confidently in the direction of his dreams, and endeavors to live the life which he has imagined, he will meet with a success unexpected in common hours.
—*Henry David Thoreau*

Hitch your wagon to a star.
—*Ralph Waldo Emerson*

Humbleness

When you're as great as I am, it's hard to be humble.
                                        —*Muhammad Ali*

If I only had a little humility, I would be perfect.
                                        —*Ted Turner*

The humblest individual exerts some influence,
    either for good or evil, upon others.
                                        —*Henry Ward Beecher*

There's a lot to be said for the fellow
    who doesn't say it himself.
                                        —*Maurice Switzer*

Do thou restrain the haughty spirit in
    thy breast, for better far is gentle courtesy.
                                        —*Homer*

I was born modest; not all over, but in spots.
                                        —*Mark Twain*

Small service is true service while it lasts:
Of humblest friends, bright creature! Scorn not one:
The daisy, by the shadow that is casts,
Protects the lingering dewdrop from the sun.
—*William Wordsworth*

Most of the trouble in the world is caused
by people wanting to be important.
—*T. S. Eliot*

The highest and most lofty trees have
the most reason to dread the thunder.
—*Charles Rollin*

Do you wish people to think well of you?
Don't speak well of yourself.
—*Blaise Pascal*

Without humility there can be no humanity.
—*John Buchan*

They are proud in humility; proud that they are not proud.
—*Robert Burton*

Be completely humble and gentle;
Be patient, bearing with one another in love.
—*adapted from Ephesians 4:2*

Common-looking people are the best in the world;
that is the reason the Lord made so many of them.
—*Abraham Lincoln*

I pray God to keep me from being proud.
—*Samuel Pepys*

I should not dare to call my soul my own.
—*Elizabeth Barrett Browning*

If I have seen further it is by standing
on the shoulders of Giants.
—*Sir Isaac Newton*

A dwarf standing on the shoulders of a
giant may see farther than a giant himself.
—*Robert Burton*

The poorest he that is in England hath
a life to live as the greatest he.
—*Thomas Rainborowe*

Whatever accomplishment you boast
of in the world, there is someone better than you.
—*African proverb*

Imagination

Imagination is more important than knowledge.
Knowledge is limited. Imagination encircles the world.
—*Albert Einstein*

To imagine is everything, to know is nothing at all.
—*Anatole France*

Imagination and fiction make up more
than three-quarters of our real life.
—*Simone Weil*

Imagination rules the world.
—*Napoleon Bonaparte*

Were it not for imagination, a man would be as
happy in the arms of a chambermaid as of a duchess.
—*Samuel Johnson*

Where I cannot satisfy my reason,
I love to humour my fancy.
—*Sir Thomas Browne*

Fantasy is the only truth.
—Abbie Hoffman

Imagination has always had powers of
resurrection that no science can match.
—Ingrid Bengis

Live out of your imagination, not your history.
—Stephen Covey

Imagination is the only weapon in the war against reality.
—Jules de Gautier

Fantasies are more than substitutes for unpleasant
reality; they are also dress rehearsals, plans. All acts
performed in the world begin in the imagination.
—Barbara Grizzuti Harrison

Imagination is the eye of the soul.
—Joseph Joubert

An idea is salvation by imagination.
—*Frank Lloyd Wright*

'I daresay you haven't had much practice,' said the
Queen. 'When I was your age, I always did it for
half-an-hour a day. Why, sometimes I've believed as
many as six impossible things before breakfast.'
—*Lewis Carroll*

Let us leave pretty women to men without imagination.
—*Marcel Proust*

The eyes are not responsible
when the mind does the seeing.
—*Publilius Syrus*

Wide and undetermined prospects are as
pleasing to the fancy, as the speculations of eternity
or infinitude are to the understanding.
—*Joseph Addison*

Imagination grows by exercise, and contrary to common belief, is more powerful in the mature than in the young.
—*W. Somerset Maugham*

A rock pile ceases to be a rock pile the moment a single man contemplates it, bearing within him the image of a cathedral.
—*Antoine de Saint Exupéry*

There is a boundary to men's passions when they act from feelings; but none when they are under the influence of imagination.
—*Edmund Burke*

Fools act on imagination without knowledge, pedants act on knowledge without imagination.
—*Alfred North Whitehead*

Journey

The journey of a thousand miles begins with one step.
>—*Lao Tzu*

If we are always arriving and departing, it is also true
that we are eternally anchored. One's destination is never
a place but rather a new way of looking at things.
>—*Henry Miller*

Make voyages. Attempt them. There's nothing else.
>—*Tennessee Williams*

Despite the success cult, men are most deeply moved
not by the reaching of the goal but by the grandness
of effort involved in getting there—or failing to get there.
>—*Max Lerner*

Perfection is a road, not a destination.
Every time I live, I get an education.
>—*Burke Hudson*

I now begin the journey that will
lead me into the sunset of my life.
—*Ronald Reagan*

Success consists in the climb.
—*Elbert Hubbard*

The real voyage of discovery consists not in
seeking new landscapes but in having new eyes.
—*Marcel Proust*

The world is a book, and those who
do not travel, read only a page.
—*St. Augustine*

To travel hopefully is a better thing than to arrive.
—*Robert Louis Stevenson*

So instead of getting to Heaven,
at last—I'm going, all along.
—*Emily Dickinson*

For my part, I travel not to go anywhere, but to go.
I travel for travel's sake. The great affair is to move.

—*Robert Louis Stevenson*

People take different roads seeking fulfillment
and happiness. Just because they're not on your
road doesn't mean they've gotten lost.

—*H. Jackson Brown, Jr.*

Writers and travelers are mesmerized
alike by knowing of their destinations.

—*Eudora Welty*

Remember that wherever you go, there you are.

—*Peter Weller*

The real meaning of travel, like that of a
conversation by the fireside, is the discovery of
oneself through contact with other people, and its
condition is self-commitment in the dialogue.

—*Paul Tournier*

When the whistle blew and the call stretched
thin across the night, one had to believe that any
journey could be sweet to the soul.
—*Charles Turner*

To find the point where hypothesis and fact meet; the
delicate equilibrium between dream and reality; the
place where fantasy and earthly things are metamorphosed
into a work of art; the house when faith in the future
becomes knowledge of the past; to lay down one's power
for others in need; to shake off the old ordeal and get
ready for the new; to question, knowing that never can
the full answer be found; to accept uncertainties quietly,
even our incomplete knowledge of God; this is what
man's journey is about, I think.
—*Lillian Smith*

All rising to great places is by a winding stair.
—*Francis Bacon*

My advice to those who are about to begin, in
earnest, the journey of life, is to take their heart
in one hand and a club in the other.
—*Josh Billings*

I'm not worldly, a bit of a savage really. I love the trees,
the isolation, the soul. I've a mystic temperament,
an independence that prevents me from constantly
looking into myself. I'm not suicidal but alive, excessive,
bloody-minded, above all a traveler without need
for medicaments to assist my journey.
—*Gérard Depardieu*

There is something about going to the sea. A little bit
of discipline, self-discipline and humility are required.
—*Prince Andrew*

Life, as the most ancient of all metaphors insists,
is a journey; and the travel book, in its deceptive
simulation of the journey's fits and starts, rehearses
life's own fragmentation. More even than the novel,
it embraces the contingency of things.
—*Jonathan Raban*

As the Spanish proverb says, 'He who would bring home
the wealth of the Indies, must carry the wealth of the
Indies with him.' So it is with traveling. A man must carry
knowledge with him if he would bring home knowledge.
—*Samuel Johnson*

Keep Ithaca always in your mind.
Arriving there is what you are destined for.
But do not hurry the journey at all.
—*C. P. Cavafy*

How much a dunce that has been sent to roam
Excels a dunce that has been kept at home!
—*William Cowper*

My favourite thing is to go where I've never been.
—*Diane Arbus*

Travel is ninety percent anticipation
and ten percent recollection.
—*Edward Streeter*

I find the great thing in this world is not so
much where we stand, as in what direction we
are moving: To reach the port of heaven, we must
sail sometimes with the wind and sometimes against it,
but we must sail, and not drift, nor lie at anchor.
—*Oliver Wendell Holmes*

He who is outside his door already has
a hard part of his journey behind him.

—Dutch proverb

Remember that happiness is a
way of travel—not a destination.

—Roy M. Goodman

He who would learn to fly one day must
first learn to stand and walk and run and
climb and dance; one cannot fly into flying.

—Friedrich Nietsche

My body has certainly wandered a good deal, but I have an
uneasy suspicion that my mind has not wandered enough.

—Noel Coward

I always love to begin a journey on Sundays, because
I shall have the prayers of the church to preserve all
that travel by land, or by water.

—Jonathan Swift

Never look down to test the ground before taking
your next step; only he who keeps his eye fixed
on the far horizon will find his right road.
—*Dag Hammarskjöld*

A man travels the world in search of
what he needs and returns home to find it.
—*George Moore*

Before he sets out, the traveler must possess fixed
interests and facilities, to be served by travel. If he drifted
aimlessly from country to country he would not travel
but only wander, ramble as a tramp. The traveler must
be somebody and come from somewhere so his definite
character and moral traditions may supply an origin and
a point of comparison for his observations.
—*George Santayana*

Justice

Justice, sir, is the great interest of man on earth.
—Daniel Webster

Without justice, courage is weak.
—Benjamin Franklin

The strictest justice is sometimes the greatest injustice.
—Terence

Justice, though due to the accused, is due to the accuser also. The concept of fairness must not be strained till it is narrowed to a filament. We are to keep the balance true.
—Benjamin Cardozo

If we do not maintain Justice, Justice will not maintain us.
—Francis Bacon

It is better that ten guilty escape than one innocent suffer.
—William Blackstone

When a just cause reaches its flood tide . . . whatever stands in the way must fall before its overwhelming power.
—*Carrie Chapman Catt*

It is easy to be popular. It is not easy to be just.
—*Rose Bird*

Fairness is what justice really is.
—*Potter Stewart*

Justice is the ligament which holds civilized beings and civilized nations together.
—*Daniel Webster*

In no sense do I advocate evading or defying the law. . . . That would lead to anarchy. An individual who breaks a law that his conscience tells him is unjust, and who willingly accepts the penalty of imprisonment in order to arouse the conscience of the community over its injustice, is in reality expressing the highest respect for law.
—*Martin Luther King, Jr.*

Justice cannot be for one side alone, but must be for both.
—*Eleanor Roosevelt*

Though force can protect in emergency, only
justice, fairness, consideration and cooperation can
finally lead men to the dawn of eternal peace.
—*Dwight D. Eisenhower*

If every man and woman and child in the world
had a chance to make a decent, fair, honest living, there
would be no jails, and no lawyers and no courts.
—*Clarence Darrow*

Nobody is poor unless he stands in need of justice.
—*Lactantius*

I would remind you that extremism in the defense of
liberty is no vice. And let me remind you also that
moderation in the pursuit of justice is no virtue.
—*Barry Goldwater*

Injustice anywhere is a threat to justice everywhere.
We are caught in an inescapable network of
mutuality, tied in a single garment of destiny.
Whatever affects one directly, affects all indirectly.
—*Martin Luther King, Jr.*

Whenever a separation is made between liberty
and justice, neither, in my opinion, is safe.
—*Edmund Burke*

Charity is no substitute for justice withheld.
—*St. Augustine*

Justice and power must be brought together,
so that whatever is just may be powerful,
and whatever is powerful may be just.
—*Blaise Pascal*

If we are to keep our democracy, there must be
one commandment: Thou shalt not ration justice.
—*Learned Hand*

Kindness

If a man be gracious and courteous to strangers,
it shows he is a citizen of the world, and that his
heart is no island cut off from other lands, but
a continent that joins to them.

—*Francis Bacon*

That best portion of a good man's life; his little,
nameless, unremembered acts of kindness and of love.

—*William Wordsworth*

You cannot do a kindness too soon because
you never know how soon it will be too late.

—*Ralph Waldo Emerson*

Kindness is wisdom.

—*Philip Bailey*

Be nice to people on your way up because
you'll meet them on your way down.

—*Wilson Mizner*

Every man feels instinctively that all the beautiful sentiments in the world weigh less than a single lovely action.

—*James Russell Lowell*

Life is not so short but that there is
always time enough for courtesy.

—*Ralph Waldo Emerson*

Therefore, however you want people to treat you,
so treat them. . . . (the Golden Rule)

—*adapted from Matthew 7:12*

And be kind to one another, tenderhearted, forgiving
each other, just as God in Christ also has forgiven you.

—*adapted from Ephesians 4:32*

Nothing is ever lost by courtesy. It is the cheapest
of the pleasures; costs nothing and conveys much.
It pleases him who gives and him who receives,
and thus, like mercy, it is twice blessed.

—*Erastus Wiman*

Human kindness has never weakened the stamina
or softened the fiber of a free people. A nation
does not have to be cruel in order to be tough.
—*Franklin D. Roosevelt*

A kind heart is a fountain of gladness, making
everything in its vicinity freshen into smiles.
—*Washington Irving*

Kindness glides about my house.
Dame Kindness, she is so nice!
The blue and red jewels of her rings smoke
In the windows, the mirrors
Are filling with smiles.
—*Sylvia Plath*

We have one simple rule here: Be kind.
—*Sam Jaffe*

Politeness is one half good nature
and the other half good lying.
—*Mary Wilson Little*

I have always depended on the kindness of strangers.
—*Vivien Leigh*

See ye not, courtesy
Is the true alchemy,
Turning to gold all it touches and tries?
—*George Meredith*

No act of kindness, however small, is ever wasted.
—*Aesop*

Kindness is a language the dumb can speak
and the deaf can hear and understand.
—*Christian Nestell Bovee*

In this world, you must be a bit too
kind in order to be kind enough.
—*Pierre Carlet*

Great persons are able to do great kindnesses.
—*Miguel de Cervantes*

Laughter & Smiles

The most wasted day of all is that
on which we have not laughed.
—*Sebastien Roch Chamfort*

Among those whom I like or admire, I can
find no common denominator, but among those
whom I love, I can: all of them make me laugh.
—*W. H. Auden*

The sound of laughter is like the
vaulted dome of a temple of happiness.
—*Milian Kundera*

If you don't learn to laugh at trouble, you
won't have anything to laugh at when you're old.
—*Edgar Watson Howe*

No man who has once heartily and wholly laughed
can be altogether irreclaimably bad.
—*Thomas Carlyle*

To laugh is proper to man.
—*François Rabelais*

I think the next best thing to solving
a problem is finding some humor in it.
—*Frank A. Clark*

Laughter is the sun that drives
winter from the human face.
—*Victor Hugo*

Seven days without laughter makes one weak.
—*Joel Goodman*

A man is not poor if he can still laugh.
—*Raymond Hitchcock*

If you have one smile in you, give it to the people you
love. Don't be surly at home, then go out in the street
and start grinning 'Good morning' at total strangers.
—*Maya Angelou*

A good laugh is sunshine in a house.
—*William Makepeace Thackeray*

Laughter is man's most distinctive emotional expression. Man shares the capacity for love and hate, anger and fear, loyalty and grief, with other living creatures. But humor, which has an intellectual as well as an emotional element, belongs to man.
—*Margaret Mead*

Wear a smile and have friends; wear a scowl and have wrinkles. What do we live for if not to make the world less difficult for each other?
—*George Eliot*

If it's sanity you're after
There's no recipe like
Laughter.
Laugh it off.
—*Henry Rutherford Elliot*

I feel an earnest and humble desire, and shall till I die, to increase the stock of harmless cheerfulness.
—*Charles Dickens*

Never stay up on the barren heights of cleverness,
but come down into the green valleys of silliness.
—*Ludwig Wittgenstein*

We are all here for a spell, get all the good laughs you can.
—*Will Rogers*

The best way to cheer yourself up
is to try to cheer somebody else up.
—*Mark Twain*

There often seems to be a playfulness to wise people,
as if either their equanimity has as its source this playfulness or the playfulness flows from the equanimity; and
they can persuade other people who are in a state of
agitation to calm down and manage a smile.
—*Edward Hoagland*

A keen sense of humor helps us to overlook the unbecom-
ing, understand the unconventional, tolerate the unpleasant, overcome the unexpected, and outlast the unbearable.
—*Billy Graham*

Smile and others will smile back.
—*Jean Baudrillard*

As happy as man as any in the world, for
the whole world seems to smile upon me.
—*Samuel Pepys*

One loses so many laughs by not laughing at oneself.
—*Sara Jeannette Duncan*

Smile at each other, smile at your wife, smile at your
husband, smile at your children, smile at each other—
it doesn't matter who it is—and that will help you to
grow up in greater love for each other.
—*Mother Teresa*

He deserves paradise who makes his companions laugh.
—*The Koran*

Laughter is the shortest distance between two people.
—*Victor Borge*

The love of truth lies at the root of much humour.
—*Robertson Davies*

Laughter is the sensation of feeling good all
over, and showing it principally in one spot.
—*Josh Billings*

So, of cheerfulness, or a good temper,
the more it is spent, the more it remains.
—*Ralph Waldo Emerson*

The most wasted of all days is one without laughter.
—*e. e. cummings*

Laughter is the closest thing to the grace of God.
—*Karl Barth*

People who laugh actually live longer than those
who don't laugh. Few persons realize that health
actually varies according to the amount of laughter.
—*James J. Walsh*

Liberty

The love of liberty is the love of others.
The love of power is the love of ourselves.
— *William Hazlitt*

He who would save liberty must
put his trust in democracy.
— *Norman Thomas*

Liberty like charity must begin at home.
— *James Bryant Conant*

A well-governed appetite is a great part of liberty.
— *Lucius Annaeus Seneca*

Experience should teach us to be most on
our guard to protect liberty when the government's
purposes are beneficial. The greatest dangers to liberty
lurk in insidious encroachment by men of zeal, well
meaning but without understanding.
— *Louis D. Brandeis*

A free spirit takes liberties even with liberty itself.
—*Francis Picabia*

Eternal vigilance is the price of liberty.
—*Thomas Jefferson*

What light is to the eyes—what air is to the lungs—
what love is to the heart, liberty is to the soul of man.
—*Robert Green Ingersoll*

The only soil in which liberty can grow is that of a
united people. We must have faith that the welfare of
one is the welfare of all. We must know that the truth
can only be reached by the expression of our free
opinions, without fear and without rancor.
—*Wendell Willkie*

It was we, the people, not we, the male citizens: but
we the whole people, who formed this Union. And
we formed it . . . to give the blessings of liberty . . . to
the whole people—women as well as men.
—*Susan B. Anthony*

Liberty trains for liberty. Responsibility
is the first step in responsibility.
—*W. E. B. Du Bois*

It is not the fact of liberty but the way in
which liberty is exercised that ultimately
determines whether liberty itself survives.
—*Dorothy Thompson*

If liberty has any meaning it means freedom to improve.
—*Philip Wylie*

The God who gave us life,
gave us liberty at the same time.
—*Thomas Jefferson*

We are as great as our belief in human liberty—
no greater. And our belief in human liberty is
only ours when it is larger than ourselves.
—*Archibald MacLeish*

Happiness must be achieved through
liberty rather than in spite of liberty.
—*Wendell Willkie*

He alone deserves liberty and life
who daily must win them anew.
—*Johann Wolfgang von Goethe*

Let every nation know, whether it wishes us well or ill,
that we shall pay any price, bear any burden, meet any
hardship, support any friend, oppose any foe to assure
the survival and the success of liberty.
—*John F. Kennedy*

Liberty is the only thing you cannot have
unless you are willing to give it to others.
—*William Allen White*

Is life so dear or peace so sweet as to be purchased
at the price of chains and slavery? Forbid it, Almighty
God! I know not what course others may take, but
as for me, give me liberty, or give me death!
—*Patrick Henry*

Liberty requires opportunity to make a living—
a living decent according to the standard of the time,
a living which gives a man not only enough to
live by, but something to live for.
—*Franklin D. Roosevelt*

When I say liberty I do not simply mean what is referred
to as 'free enterprise.' I mean liberty of the individual
to think his own thoughts and live his own life as he
desires to think and to live; the liberty of the family to
decide how they wish to live, what they want to eat for
breakfast and for dinner, and how they wish to spend
their time; liberty of a man to develop his ideas and
get other people to teach those ideas, if he can convince
them that they have some value to the world; liberty
of every local community to decide how its children shall
be educated; how its local services shall be run, and who
its local leaders shall be; liberty of a man to choose his own
occupation; and liberty of a man to run his own business
as he thinks it ought to be run, as long as he does not
interfere with the rights of other people to do the same thing.
—*Robert A. Taft*

Where liberty is, there is my country.
—*James Otis*

The spirit of liberty is the spirit which is not too sure
that it is right; the spirit of liberty is the spirit which
seeks to understand the minds of other men and women;
the spirit of liberty is the spirit which weighs their interests
alongside its own without bias; the spirit of liberty remem-
bers that not even a sparrow falls to earth unheeded;
the spirit of liberty is the spirit of Him who, nearly two
thousand years ago, taught mankind that lesson it has
never learned, but has never quite forgotten: that there
is a kingdom where the least shall be heard and
considered side by side with the greatest.

—*Learned Hand*

We knew thee of old,
O divinely restored,
By the light of thine eyes
And the light of thy sword.
From the graves of our slain
Shall thy valor prevail
As we greet thee again—
Hail, Liberty! Hail!

—*Dionysios Solomos*

The cost of liberty is less than the price of repression.

—*W. E. B. Du Bois*

Life

Would that life were like the shadow cast by a wall
or a tree, but it is like the shadow of a bird in flight.
—*The Talmud*

Next to knowing when to seize an
opportunity, the most important thing in
life is to know when to forgo an advantage.
—*Benjamin Disraeli*

Life is consciousness.
—*Emmet Fox*

Live all you can; it's a mistake not to.
It doesn't so much matter what you do
in particular so long as you have your life.
—*Henry James*

There are three indgredients in the
good life; learning, earning, and yearning.
—*Christopher Morley*

Life is—or has—meaning and
meaninglessness. I cherish the anxious hope
that meaning will preponderate and win the battle.
—*Carl Jung*

Life is a loom, weaving illusion.
—*Vachel Lindsay*

We are here to add what we can to life,
not to get what we can from it.
—*William Osler*

Life, you know, is rather like opening a tin
of sardines. We're all of us looking for the key.
—*Alan Bennett*

Life is a long lesson in humility.
—*James M. Barrie*

If you don't run your own life, somebody else will.
—*John Atkinson*

Life has a practice of living you if you don't live it.
—*Philip Larkin*

I can't think of a more wonderful
thanksgiving for the life I have had than
that everyone should be jolly at my funeral.
—*Earl Mountbatten of Burma*

It is not the years in your life
but the life in your years that counts.
—*Adlai Stevenson*

What is life? It is the flash of a firefly in the night. It is the
breath of a buffalo in the wintertime. It is the little shadow
which runs across the grass and loses itself in the sunset.
—*Crowfoot*

Our horizon is never quite at our elbows.
—*Henry David Thoreau*

Life is ours to be spent, not to be saved.
—*D. H. Lawrence*

Let us so live that when we come
to die even the undertaker will be sorry.
—*Mark Twain*

All men should strive to learn before they die
what they are running from, and to, and why.
—*James Thurber*

The true meaning of life is to plant trees,
under whose shade you do not expect to sit.
—*Nelson Henderson*

All of life is a foreign country.
—*Jack Kerouac*

Tomorrow's life is too late. Live today.
—*Marcus Valerius Martialis*

Life is action and passion; therefore, it is required
of a man that he should share the passions and action
of the time, at peril of being judged not to have lived.
—*Oliver Wendell Holmes*

Life is what happens to you while
you're busy making other plans.
—*John Lennon*

Life is not a dress rehearsal.
—*Rose Tremain*

The great business of life is to be,
to do, to do without and to depart.
—*John Morley*

Do not take life too seriously—
you will never get out of it alive.
—*Elbert Hubbard*

One lives but once in the world.
—*Johann Wolfgang von Goethe*

I love a broad margin to my life.
—*Henry David Thoreau*

If there is another world, he lives in bliss.
If there is none, he made the best of this.
—*Robert Burns*

Variety's the very spice of life.
—*William Cowper*

He who would teach men
to die would teach them to live.
—*Michel E. de Montaigne*

I went to the woods because I wished to live
deliberately, to front only the essential facts of life,
and see if I could not learn what it had to teach, and not,
which I came to die, discover that I had not lived.
—*Henry David Thoreau*

Three passions, simple but overwhelmingly
strong, have governed my life; the longing for
love, the search for knowledge, and unbearable
pity for the suffering of mankind.
—*Bertrand Russell*

Our greatest danger in life is in permitting
the urgent things to crowd out the important.
—*Oliver Wendell Holmes*

It is better to be than not to be.
—*Aristotle*

There'll be two dates on your tombstone
And all your friends will read 'em
But all that's gonna matter is that little dash between 'em ...
—*Kevin Welch*

Life is not a matter of place, things or comfort;
rather, it concerns the basic human rights
of family, country, justice and human dignity.
—*Imelda Marcos*

Do not fear death so much, but rather the inadequate life.
—*Bertolt Brecht*

Life consists in what a man is thinking of all day.
—*Ralph Waldo Emerson*

And life is what we make it.
Always has been, always will be.
—*Grandma Moses*

So one thing I want to say about life is don't be
scared and don't hang back, and most of all, don't waste it.
—*Joan W. Blos*

My trade and my art is living.
—*Michel E. de Montaigne*

There is no such thing in anyone's
life as an unimportant day.
—*Alexander Woollcott*

We live, not as we wish to, but as we can.
—*Menander*

The great use of life is to spend it
for something that will outlast it.
—*William James*

There is no cure for birth and death,
save to enjoy the interval.
—*George Santayana*

Life is uncertain. Eat dessert first.
—*Ernestine Ulmer*

Life is an opportunity, benefit from it.
Life is beauty, admire it.
Life is bliss, taste it.
Life is a dream, realize it.
Life is a challenge, meet it.
Life is a duty, complete it.
Life is a game, play it.
Life is a promise, fulfill it.
Life is sorrow, overcome it.
Life is a song, sing it.
Life is a struggle, accept it.
Life is a tragedy, confront it.
Life is an adventure, dare it.
Life is luck, make it.
Life is too precious, do not destroy it.
Life is life, fight for it.
—*Mother Teresa*

That it will never come again
Is what makes life so sweet.
—*Emily Dickinson*

Each man must look to himself to teach him
the meaning of life. It is not something discovered;
it is something moulded.
—*Antoine de Saint Exupéry*

Be a life long or short, its completeness
depends on what it was lived for.
—*David Starr Jordan*

May you live all the days of your life.
—*Jonathan Swift*

The actuality of thought is life.
—*Aristotle*

We learn the rope of life by untying its knots.
—*Jean Toomer*

The great art of life is sensation,
to feel that we exist, even in pain.

—*Lord Byron*

Common sense and nature will do a lot
to make the pilgrimage of life not too difficult.

—*W. Somerset Maugham*

You only live once—but if you
work it right, once is enough.

—*Joe E. Lewis*

Life can only be understood backwards;
but it must be lived forwards.

—*Soren Kierkegaard*

Life is an unanswered question, but let's still believe
in the dignity and importance of the question.

—*Tennessee Williams*

Strange as it may seem, my life is based on a true story.

—*Ashleigh Brilliant*

277

A man has made at least a start on discovering
the meaning of human life when he plants shade
trees under which he knows full well he will never sit.
—*D. Elton Trueblood*

The science of life . . . is a superb and dazzlingly
lighted hall which may be reached only by passing
through a long and ghastly kitchen.
—*Claude Bernard*

I look upon life as a gift from God. I did
nothing to earn it. Now that the time is coming
to give it back, I have no right to complain.
—*Joyce Cary*

Limitless Possibilities

The great law of culture is: Let each become
all that he was created capable of being.
—*Thomas Carlyle*

We never know how high we are
Till we are called to rise
And then, if we are true to plan
Our statures touch the skies.
—*Emily Dickinson*

You commit a sin of omission if you
do not utilize all the power that is within you.
—*Oliver Wendell Holmes*

That's one small step for man, one giant leap for mankind.
—*Neil Armstrong*

You never know what you can do until you have to do it.
—*Betty Ford*

Some of the world's greatest feats were accomplished by people not smart enough to know they were impossible.
—*Doug Larson*

Nothing is impossible; there are ways that lead to everything, and if we had sufficient will we should always have sufficient means. It is often merely for an excuse that we say things are impossible.
—*François de la Rochefoucauld*

Even a good idea may run wild in an open and empty mind.
—*Herbert V. Prochnow*

To me every hour of the light and dark is a miracle, Every cubic inch of space is a miracle.
—*Walt Whitman*

The only way to discover the limits of the possible is to go beyond them into the impossible.
—*Arthur C. Clarke*

The Age of Miracles is forever here!
—*Thomas Carlyle*

Our problems are man-made, therefore they may be
solved by man. And man can be as big as he wants.
No problem of human destiny is beyond human beings.
—*John F. Kennedy*

The difference between what we do and
what we are capable of doing would suffice
to solve most of the world's problems.
—*Gandhi*

I know of no more encouraging fact than
the unquestionable ability of man to elevate
his life by a conscious endeavor.
—*Henry David Thoreau*

Never exceed your rights, and they
will soon become unlimited.
—*Jean-Jacques Rousseau*

The great pleasure in life is doing
what people say you cannot do.
—*Walter Bagehot*

Nothing is improbably until it moves into the past tense.
—*George Ade*

The Difficult is that which can be done immediately;
the Impossible that which takes a little longer.
—*George Santayana*

Most of the things worth doing in the world
had been declared impossible before they were done.
—*Louis D. Brandeis*

In the country of the blind, the one-eyed man is king.
—*Desiderius Erasmus*

What small potatoes we all are,
compared with what we might be!
—*Charles Dudley Warner*

Love

Whoever lov'd that lov'd not at first sight?
—*William Shakespeare*

The greatest determiner of human happiness is whether
or not we have someone to love and confide in.
—*Joyce Brothers*

I don't want to live—I want to love first,
and live incidentally.
—*Zelda Fitzgerald*

Oh, 'tis love, 'tis love that makes the world go round.
—*Lewis Carroll*

To be loved, be lovable.
—*Ovid*

Love does not consist in gazing at each other,
but in looking together in the same direction.
—*Antoine de Saint Exupéry*

This is My commandment, that you
love one another, just as I have loved you.
—*adapted from John 15:12*

You shall not take vengeance, nor bear any
grudge against the sons of your people, but you
shall love your neighbor as yourself; I am the Lord.
—*adapted from Leviticus 19:18*

Love gives itself; it is not bought.
—*Henry Wadsworth Longfellow*

The pleasure of love is in loving. We are happier
in the passion we feel than in that we inspire.
—*Françios de la Rochefoucauld*

To love is to place our happiness
in the happiness of others.
—*Gottfried Wilhelm von Leibniz*

Familiar acts are beautiful through love.
—*Percy Bysshe Shelley*

Love means giving one's self to another person fully,
not just physically. When two people really love each
other, this helps them to stay alive and grow. One must
really be loved to grow. Love's such a precious and
fragile thing that when it comes we have to hold on
tightly. And when it comes, we're very lucky because
for some it never comes at all. If you have love, you're
wealthy in a way that can never be measured. Cherish it.
—*Nancy Reagan*

We love the things we love for what they are.
—*Robert Frost*

Real love is a pilgrimage. It happens
when there is no strategy, but it is very rare
because most people are strategists.
—*Anita Brookner*

The truth is that there is only one terminal dignity—love.
And the story of a love is not important—what
is important is that one is capable of love. It is perhaps
the only glimpse we are permitted of eternity.
—*Helen Hayes*

If we all discovered that we had only five minutes
left to say all the things we wanted to say, every
telephone booth would be occupied by people
calling other people to tell them that they loved them.
—*Christopher Morley*

Love is everything it's cracked up to be. That's why
people are so cynical about it. . . . It really is worth
fighting for, being brave for, risking everything for. And
the trouble is, if you don't risk anything, you risk even more.
—*Erica Jong*

We can only learn to love by loving.
—*Iris Murdoch*

Earth's the right place for love: I don't
know where it's likely to go better.
—*Robert Frost*

Darkness cannot drive out darkness; only light can do that.
Hate cannot drive out hate; only love can do that.
—*Martin Luther King, Jr.*

Love is the life of the soul.
It is the harmony of the universe.
—*William Ellery Channing*

Love is spiritual fire.
—*Emanuel Swedenborg*

The love we give away is the only love we keep.
—*Elbert Hubbard*

One does not fall into love; one grows
into love, and love grows in him.
—*Karl Menninger*

The emotion of love, in spite of the romantics, is not
self-sustaining; it endures only when the lovers love
many things together, and not merely each other.
—*Walter Lippmann*

I never knew how to worship until I knew how to love.
—*Henry Ward Beecher*

A coward is incapable of exhibiting love;
it is the prerogative of the brave.

—*Gandhi*

Love is the triumph of imagination over intelligence.

—*H. L. Mencken*

Love yourself first and everything else falls into line.

—*Lucille Ball*

Love doesn't just sit there, like a stone, it has to
be made, like bread; re-made all the time, made new.

—*Ursula K. Le Guin*

When one loves somebody, everything is clear—
where to go, what to do—it all takes care of itself
and one doesn't have to ask anybody about anything.

—*Maxim Gorky*

It is a wonderful seasoning of all
enjoyments to think of those we love.

—*Molière*

Love is the irresistible desire to be desired irresistibly.
—*Louis Ginsberg*

Love consists in this, that two solitudes
protect and touch and greet each other.
—*Rainer Maria Rilke*

The birthday of my life
Is come, my love is come to me.
—*Christina Georgina Rossetti*

Love, and do what you like.
—*St. Augustine*

We always love those who admire us; we
do not always love those whom we admire.
—*François de la Rochefoucauld*

From success you get a lot of things, but
not that great inside thing that love brings you.
—*Sam Goldwyn*

Nothing is menial where there is love.
—*Pearl S. Buck*

Love is an act of endless forgiveness,
a tender look which becomes a habit.
—*Peter Ustinov*

Two souls with but a single thought,
Two hearts that beat as one.
—*Friedrich Halm*

She whom I love is hard to catch and conquer,
Hard, but O the glory of the winning were she won!
—*George Meredith*

Immature love says "I love you because I need you."
Mature love says "I need you because I love you."
—*Erich Fromm*

To live is like to love—all reason
is against it, and all healthy instinct for it.
—*Samuel Butler*

To be able to say how much you love is to love but little.
—*Petrarch*

I've decided to stick with love.
Hate is too great a burden to bear.
—*Martin Luther King, Jr.*

Who can give law to lovers? Love is a greater law to itself.
—*Boethius*

One word
Frees us of all the weight and pain of life:
That word is love.
—*Sophocles*

Every man loves what he is good at.
—*Thomas Shadwell*

Love has always been the most important
business in my life, I should say the only one.
—*Stendhal*

In peace, Love tunes the shepherd's reed;
In war, he mounts the warrior's steed;
In halls, in gay attire is seen;
In hamlets, dances on the green.
Love rules the court, the camp, the grove,
And men below, and saints above;
For love is heaven, and heaven is love.
—*Sir Walter Scott*

O, human love! thou spirit given,
On Earth, of all we hope in Heaven!
—*Edgar Allan Poe*

Love conquers all things; let us too surrender to Love.
—*Virgil*

The final cause, then, produces
motion though being loved.
—*Aristotle*

All mankind love a lover.
—*Ralph Waldo Emerson*

Love seeketh not itself to please,
Nor for itself hath any care,
But for another gives its ease,
And builds a Heaven in Hell's despair.
—*William Blake*

No love, no friendship can cross the path of our
destiny without leaving some mark on it forever.
—*François Mauriac*

The secret of a happy home life is that the members
of the family learn to give and receive love.
—*Billy Graham*

Passion is a sort of fever in the mind, which
ever heaves us weaker than it found us.
—*William Penn*

But true love is a durable fire,
In the mind ever burning,
Never sick, never old, never dead,
From itself never turning.
—*Sir Walter Raleigh*

But there's nothing half so sweet in life
As love's young dream.

—*Thomas Moore*

'Tis better to have loved and lost
Than never to have loved at all.

—*Lord Tennyson*

Of all forms of caution, caution in love is
perhaps the most fatal to true happiness.

—*Bertrand Russell*

The supreme happiness of life
is the conviction that we are loved.

—*Victor Hugo*

But now abide faith, hope, love, these three;
but the greatest of these is love.

—*adapted from 1 Corinthians 13:13*

Nature

The year's at the spring
And day's at the morn;
Morning's at seven;
The hillside's dew-pearled;
The lark's on the wing;
The snail's on the thorn:
God's in his heaven –
All's right with the world.

—*Robert Browning*

The ignorant man marvels at the exceptional;
the wise man marvels at the common; the greatest
wonder of all is the regularity of nature.

—*George Dana Boardman*

The least movement is of importance to all nature.
The entire ocean is affected by a pebble.

—*Blaise Pascal*

The poetry of earth is never dead.

—*John Keats*

Snowflakes are one of nature's most fragile things,
but just look what they can do when they stick together.
—*Vesta M. Kelly*

The most important outside influence in my life
was the river, the Mississippi. I can't imagine what I
might have been in mind and temperament had
I not grown up with the river. Landscape has always
meant more to me than people, and while for most
of my adult life I have been a mountain woman, the
river is still the background of my thoughts and emotions.
—*Mary Meigs Atwater*

Tall poplars—human beings of this earth!
—*Paul Celan*

Our task is not to rediscover nature but to remake it.
—*Raoul Vaneigem*

The sun, though it passes through dirty
places, yet remains as pure as before.
—*Francis Bacon*

The ocean and I have many pebbles
To find and wash off and roll into shape.
—*William Stafford*

———•———

For whatever we lose (like a you or a me)
it's always ourselves we find in the sea.
—*e. e. cummings*

———•———

The most beautiful thing under
the sun is being under the sun.
—*Christa Wolf*

———•———

A poor woman from Manchester, on being
taken to the seaside, is said to have expressed her
delight on seeing for the first time something
of which there was enough for everybody.
—*John Lubbock*

———•———

'Look at the clouds,' Alessandro said. 'They pass so
gently and so quietly, but as if with such resolution.
Someone once said they were rafts for the souls.'
—*Mark Helprin*

297

The sun is coming down to earth, and the fields
and the waters shout to him golden shouts.

—*George Meredith*

Sunshine is delicious, rain is refreshing, wind braces up,
snow is exhilarating; there is no such thing as bad weather,
only different kinds of good weather.

—*John Ruskin*

I liked to sail alone. The sea was the same
as a girl to me—I did not want anyone else along.

—*E. B. White*

I am glad I shall never be young without wild
country to be young in. Of what avail are forty
freedoms without a blank spot of the map?

—*Aldo Leopold*

I love to think of nature as an unlimited
broadcasting station, through which God speaks
to us every hour, if we only will tune in.

—*George Washington Carver*

Everything in nature invites
us constantly to be what we are.
—*Gretel Ehrlich*

The sea possesses a power over one's moods
that has the effect of a will. The sea can hypnotize.
Nature in general can do so.
—*Henrik Ibsen*

My heart and I lie small upon
the earth like a grain of throbbing sand.
—*Zitkala-Sa*

After a debauch of thundershower, the weather
takes the pledge and signs it with a rainbow.
—*Thomas Bailey Aldrich*

We are rooted to the air through our lungs
and to the soil through our stomachs. We are
walking trees and floating plants.
—*John Burroughs*

To be head-taut with the stars around you,
foot secure on soil and stone, to know your
direction and return through outer signs, is as new
as it is ancient. We are still people of the planet,
with all its original directions waiting in our being.

—*John Hay*

The sea is calm to-night,
The tide is full, the moon lies fair
Upon the straits . . .
For the world, which seems
To lie before us like a land of dreams.

—*Matthew Arnold*

We simply need that wild country available to us, even
if we never do more than drive to its edge and look in.
For it can be a means of reassuring ourselves of our
sanity as creatures, a part of the geography of hope.

—*Wallace Stegner*

Like a gardener, I believe that
what goes down must come up.

—*Lynwood L. Giacomini*

Conservation is a state of harmony between men and land.
—Aldo Leopold

———•———

The long fight to save wild beauty represents
democracy at its best. It requires citizens to
practice the hardest of virtues—self-restraint.
—Edwin Way Teale

———•———

Everybody needs beauty as well as bread, places
to play in and pray in, where Nature may heal and
cheer and give strength to body and soul alike.
—John Muir

———•———

If I were to name the three most precious
resources of life, I should say books, friends,
and nature; and the greatest of these, at least the
most constant and always at hand, is nature.
—John Burroughs

———•———

What nature delivers to us is never stale.
Because what nature creates has eternity in it.
—Isaac Bashevis Singer

I like trees because they seem more resigned to the way
they have to live than other things do.
—*Willa Cather*

The sky is the daily bread of the eyes.
—*Ralph Waldo Emerson*

Give me a spark o' nature's fire,
That's a' the learning I desire.
—*Robert Burns*

We cannot command Nature except by obeying her.
—*Francis Bacon*

Grass is the forgiveness of nature—her
constant benediction. Forests decay, harvests
perish, flowers vanish, but grass is immortal.
—*Brian Ingalls*

The course of nature is the art of God.
—*Edward Young*

I frequently tramped eight or ten miles through the
deepest snow to keep an appointment with a beech tree,
or a yellow birch, or an old acquaintance among the pines.
—*Henry David Thoreau*

When the oak is felled the whole forest
echoes with its fall, but a hundred acorns are
sown in silence by an unnoticed breeze.
—*Thomas Carlyle*

Nature never did betray the heart that loved her.
—*William Wadsworth*

I am at two with nature.
—*Woody Allen*

Where'er you walk, cool gales shall fan the glad,
Trees, where you sit, shall crowd into a shade:
Where'er you tread, the blushing flow'rs shall rise,
And all things flourish where you turn your eyes.
—*Alexander Pope*

Keep to moderation, keep the end in view, follow nature.
—*Lucan*

Praise the sea; on shore remain.
—*John Florio*

A little garden in which to walk, an immensity in which
to dream, at one's feet that which can be cultivated and
plucked; overhead that which one can study and meditate
upon; some herbs on earth and all the stars in the sky.
—*Victor Hugo*

A rose is sweeter in the bud than full-blown.
—*John Lyly*

I must go seek some dew drops here,
And hang a pearl in every cowslip's ear.
—*William Shakespeare*

There's never an end for the sea.
—*Samuel Beckett*

Come forth into the light of things,
Let Nature be your teacher.
—*William Wordsworth*

Many stokes overthrow the tallest oaks.
—*John Lyly*

You are a child of the universe no less than
the trees and the stars; you have a right to be here.
—*Max Ehrmann*

To see the world in a grain of sand,
and heaven in a wildflower,
Hold infinity in the palm of your hand,
and eternity in an hour.
—*William Blake*

I believe a leaf of grass is no less
than the journey-work on the stars.
—*Walt Whitman*

Nature, to be commanded, must be obeyed.
—*Francis Bacon*

The goal of life is living in agreement with nature.
—*Zeno*

Nothing happens to anybody which
he is not fitted by nature to bear.
—*Marcus Aurelius Antoninus*

In all things of nature there is something of the marvelous.
—*Aristotle*

Deep in their roots,
All flowers keep the light.
—*Theodore Roethke*

Let us give Nature a chance; she
knows her business better than we do.
—*Michel E. de Montaigne*

Optimism

Both read the Bible day and night,
But thou read'st black where I read white.
—*William Blake*

A man he seems of cheerful yesterdays
And confident tomorrows.
—*William Wordsworth*

She would rather light a candle than curse
the darkness, and her glow has warmed the world.
—*Adlai Stevenson*

Rosiness is not a worse windowpane
than gloomy gray when viewing the world.
—*Grace Paley*

Be glad of life, because it gives you the chance to love
and to work and to play and to look up at the stars.
—*Henry van Dyke*

An inexhaustible good nature is one of the
most precious gifts of heaven, spreading itself like
oil over the troubled sea of thought, and keeping
the mind smooth and equable in the roughest weather.
—*Washington Irving*

All is for the best in the best of possible worlds.
—*Voltaire*

Positive anything is better than negative nothing.
—*Elbert Hubbard*

No day is so bad it can't be fixed with a nap.
—*Carrie Snow*

There is strong shadow where there is much light.
—*Johann Wolfgang von Goethe*

It is always darkest just before the day dawneth.
—*Thomas Fuller*

The habit of looking on the bright side of every
event is worth more than a thousand pounds a year.
—*Samuel Johnson*

Still round the corner there may wait
A new road, or a secret gate.
—*J. R. R. Tolkien*

Every exit is an entry somewhere.
—*Tom Stoppard*

The American, by nature, is optimistic. He is
experimental, an inventor and a builder who
builds best when called upon to build greatly.
—*John F. Kennedy*

I am still determined to be cheerful and happy in whatever
situation I may be, for I have also learned from experience
that the greater part of our happiness or misery depends
on our dispositions and not our circumstances.
—*Martha Washington*

If you suffer, thank God!—it is
a sure sign that you are alive.

—*Elbert Hubbard*

The happy ending is our national belief.

—*Mary McCarthy*

If you have a lemon, make lemonade.

—*Howard Gossage*

Never despair.

—*Horace*

There is a secret person undamaged in every individual.

—*Paul Shepard*

With all its sham, drudgery and broken
dreams, it is still a beautiful world.

—*Max Ehrmann*

I am as bad as the worst, but, thank
God, I am as good as the best.
—*Walt Whitman*

Sloppy, raggedy-assed old life. I love it. I never want to die.
—*Dennis Trudell*

There is no personal charm so great
as the charm of a cheerful temperament.
—*Henry van Dyke*

Who would have thought my shrivel'd heart
Could have recovered greenness?
—*George Herbert*

The most delightful advantage of being
bald—one can hear snowflakes.
—*R. G. Daniels*

If way to the Better there be,
it exacts a full look at the Worst.
—*Thomas Hardy*

Though my soul may set in darkness, it will rise
in perfect light,
I have loved the stars too fondly to be fearful
of the night.
—*Sarah Williams*

I'll turn over a new leaf.
—*Miguel de Cervantes*

The things we think are the things that feed our souls.
If we think on pure and lovely things, we shall grow pure
and lovely like them; and the converse is equally true.
—*Hannah Whitall Smith*

I have tried to in my time to be a philosopher; but
I don't know how, cheerfulness was always breaking in.
—*Oliver Edwards*

In these times you have to be an optimist
to open your eyes in the morning.
—*Carl Sandburg*

A brave world, sir, full of religion, knavery,
and change: we shall shortly see better days.
—*Aphra Behn*

Goodbye is always hello to something else.
—*George Ella Lyons*

Look not thou down but up!
—*Robert Browning*

Stay positive and stay on top of things.
—*Gary Paulsen*

Let other pens dwell on guilt and misery.
I quit such odious subjects as soon as I can.
—*Jane Austen*

If you think you can, you can.
And if you think you can't, you're right.
—*Mary Kay Ash*

What a glorious morning for America!
—*Samuel Adams*

When it is dark enough, you can see the stars.
—*Charles A. Beard*

After a storm comes a calm.
—*Matthew Henry*

There is not enough darkness in all the world
to put out the light of even one small candle.
—*Robert Alden*

When things come to the worst, they generally mend.
—*Susanna Moodie*

Aerodynamically, the bumble bee shouldn't
be able to fly, but the bumble bee doesn't know
it so it goes on flying anyway.
—*Mary Kay Ash*

Parenthood

The hand that rocks the cradle
Is the hand that rules the world.
—William Ross Wallace

Men are what their mothers made them.
—Ralph Waldo Emerson

Wise parents begin the process of becoming loving
authority figures during the first days of their child's life.
—Jim and Charles Fay

We spend the first twelve months of our children's
lives teaching them to walk and talk and the next
twelve telling them to sit down and shut up.
—Phyllis Diller

We have to give children opportunities to
make decisions, to give love and service until
they know how to do it on their own.
—Dwan Young

What the vast majority of American children need
is to stop being pampered, stop being indulged, stop
being chauffeured, stop being catered to. In the final
analysis it is not what you do for your children
but what you have taught them to do for themselves
that will make them successful human beings.

—*Ann Landers*

As a parent, your job is to try and fix things. But then
you have to realize that you can't control who your
children are, or what they want to do with their lives.

—*Cher*

There are no illegitimate children—
only illegitimate parents.

—*Leon R. Yankwich*

Of all the rights of women, the greatest is to be a mother.

—*Lin Yutang*

No matter how old a mother is, she watches
her middle-aged children for signs of improvement.

—*Florida Scott-Maxwell*

We never know the love of a parent
till we become parents ourselves.
—*Henry Ward Beecher*

A boy's best friend is his mother.
—*Anthony Perkins in* Psycho

We can't form our children on our own concepts;
we must take them and love them as God gives them to us.
—*Johann Wolfgang von Goethe*

Strange as it seems, children wind up making far
fewer mistakes when we no longer fear that they will.
—*Jim and Charles Fay*

The most important thing a father can do
for his children is to love their mother.
—*Theodore Hesburgh*

Children need love, especially when they do not deserve it.
—*Harold S. Hulbert*

Questions cause children to think.
Commands cause children to resist.
—*Jim and Charles Fay*

When you have kids late in life, you appreciate
them more. They keep you young, and you see the
world through better eyes. You can give your children
a finer sense of values, too, because if you're lucky,
your own values have improved with time.
—*Lucille Ball*

What the world needs is not romantic lovers who
are sufficient unto themselves, but husbands and
wives who live in communities, relate to other
people, carry on useful work and willingly give
time and attention to their children.
—*Margaret Mead*

One father is more than 100 schoolmasters.
—*George Herbert*

All that I am, or hope to be, I owe to my angel mother.
—*Abraham Lincoln*

God knows that a mother needs fortitude and courage and
tolerance and flexibility and patience and firmness and nearly
every other brave aspect of the human soul. But because I
happen to be a parent of almost fiercely maternal nature,
I praise casualness. It seems to me the rarest of virtues. It is
useful enough when children are small. It is important to
the point of necessity when they are adolescents.

—*Phillis McGinley*

Humans are the only animals that have children on
purpose with the exception of guppies, who like to eat
theirs.

—*P. J. O'Rourke*

A mother is not a person to lean on but
a person to make leaning unnecessary.

—*Dorothy Canfield Fisher*

Bringing up a family should be an adventure,
not an anxious discipline in which everybody
is constantly graded for performance.

—*Milton R. Sapirstein*

More than in any other human relationship,
overwhelmingly more, motherhood means being
instantly interruptible, responsive, responsible.
—*Tillie Olsen*

It doesn't matter who my father was;
it matters who I remembered he was.
—*Anne Sexton*

When motherhood becomes the fruit of a deep
yearning, not the result of ignorance or accident,
its children will become the foundation of a new race.
—*Margaret Sanger*

She discovered with great delight that one does not
love one's children just because they are one's children
but because of the friendship formed while raising them.
—*Gabriel Garcia Màrquez*

To bring up a child in the way he should go,
travel that way yourself once in a while.
—*Josh Billings*

Healthy bonding requires both love and limits.
—*Jim and Charles Fay*

Childbirth is more admirable than conquest, more
amazing than self-defense, and as courageous as either one.
—*Gloria Steinem*

It is not enough for parents to understand children. They
must accord children the privilege of understanding them.
—*Milton R. Sapirstein*

It's a wonderful feeling when your father becomes not
a god but a man to you—when he comes down from
the mountain and you see he's this man with weaknesses.
And you love him as this whole being, not as a figurehead.
—*Robin Williams*

Everyone likes to think that he has done reasonably
well in life, so that it comes to a shock to find our
children believing differently. The temptation is to
tune them out; it takes much more courage to listen.
—*John D. Rockefeller III*

The best brought-up children are those
who have seen their parents as they are.
Hypocrisy is not the parents' first duty.
—*George Bernard Shaw*

Mother is the name for God in the lips and hearts of children.
—*William Makepeace Thackeray*

Nothing you do for children is ever wasted.
—*Garrison Keillor*

Whatever you would have your children become,
strive to exhibit in your own lives and conversations.
—*Lydia H. Sigourney*

Your children need your presence more than your presents.
—*Jesse Jackson*

It behooves a father to be blameless
if he expects his son to be.

—*Homer*

Patience

The strongest of all warriors
are these two—Time and Patience.
—*Leo Tolstoy*

There is a strength of quiet endurance as significant
of courage as the most daring feats of prowess.
—*Henry Theodore Tuckerman*

Patience and passage of time
do more than strength and fury.
—*Jean de la Fontaine*

Genius is nothing but a greater aptitude for patience.
—*Comte de Buffon*

Our real blessings often appear to us
in the shapes of pains, losses and disappointments;
but let us have patience,
and we soon shall see them in their proper figures.
—*Joseph Addison*

Still achieving, still pursuing, learn to labor and to wait.
—*Henry Wadsworth Longfellow*

Patience, that blending of moral
courage with physical timidity.
—*Thomas Hardy*

The universe is full of magical things,
patiently waiting for our wits to grow sharper.
—*Eden Phillpotts*

Adopt the pace of nature: her secret is patience.
—*Ralph Waldo Emerson*

The trees that are slow to grow bear the best fruit.
—*Molière*

Never think that God's delays are God's denials.
Hold on; hold fast; hold out. Patience is genius.
—*Comte de Buffon*

Endurance is patience concentrated.
—*Thomas Carlyle*

He that can have patience can have what he will.
—*Benjamin Franklin*

Have patience with all things, but chiefly have
patience with yourself. Do not lose courage in
considering your own imperfections, but instantly set
about remedying them—every day being the task anew.
—*St. Francis de Sales*

There is nothing so bitter, that a patient
mind cannot find some solace for it.
—*Lucius Annaeus Seneca*

The end of a matter is better than its beginning;
patience of spirit is better than haughtiness of spirit.
—*adapted from Ecclesiastes 7:8*

Patience and time do more than strength or passion.
—*Jean de la Fontaine*

Patience is the best remedy for every trouble.
—*Titus Maccius Plautus*

Don't be overwhelmed . . . take it
one day and one prayer at a time.
—*Stormie Omartian*

They also serve who only stand and wait.
—*John Milton*

But patience, cousin, and shuffle the cards,
till our hand is a stronger one.
—*Sir Walter Scott*

Never cut what you can untie.
—*Joseph Joubert*

You must first have a lot of
patience to learn to have patience.
—*Stanislaw J. Lec*

Patriotism

A man's country is not a certain area of land,
of mountains, rivers, and woods, but it is a principle;
and patriotism is loyalty to that principle.
—*George William Curtis*

What pity is it
That we can die but once to serve our country!
—*Joseph Addison*

Up, men, and to your posts! Don't forget
today that you are from Old Virginia.
—*George Edward Pickett*

I only regret that I have
but one life to give for my country.
—*Nathan Hale*

I vow to thee, my country—all earthly things above—
Entire and whole and perfect, the service of my love.
—*Sir Cecil Spring-Rice*

Patriotism is easy to understand in America; it means looking out for yourself by looking out for your country.
—*Calvin Coolidge*

There is a higher form of patriotism than nationalism, and that higher form is not limited by the boundaries of one's country; but by a duty to mankind to safeguard the trust of civilization.
—*Oscar S. Strauss*

What we need are critical lovers of America—patriots who express their faith in their country by working to improve it.
—*Hubert H. Humphrey*

Citizenship consists in the service of a country.
—*Jawaharlal Nehru*

Patriotism is not short, frenzied outbursts of emotion, but the tranquil and steady dedication of a lifetime.
—*Adlai Stevenson*

Intellectually I know that America is no
better than any other country; emotionally
This I would say, standing as I do in view of God and
Eternity: I realize that patriotism is not enough: I must
have no hatred and bitterness towards anyone.
—*Edith Cavell*

A man's feet must be planted in his country,
but his eyes should survey the world.
—*George Santayana*

Behind all these men you have to do with, behind
officers, and government, and people even, there is
the country herself, your country and . . . you belong
to her as you belong to your own mother. Stand
by her, boy, as you would stand by your mother.
—*Edward Everett Hale*

My kind of loyalty was loyalty to one's country, not to
its institutions or its officeholders. The country is the real
thing, the substantial thing, the eternal thing; it is the
thing to watch over, and care for, and be loyal to.
—*Mark Twain*

Each man must for himself alone decide what is right
and what is wrong, which course is patriotic and
which isn't. You cannot shirk this and be a man.

—*Mark Twain*

To be radical is, in the best and only
decent sense of the word, patriotic.

—*Michael Harrington*

Our country, right or wrong. When right,
to be kept right; when wrong, to be put right.

—*Carl Schurz*

I look upon the world as my fatherland . . .
I look upon true patriotism as the brotherhood
of man and the service of all to all.

—*Helen Keller*

Open my heart, and you will see
Graved inside of it, "Italy."

—*Robert Browning*

Unless you can find some sort of loyalty, you cannot
find unity and peace in your active living.

—*Josiah Royce*

Patriotism to me was not something static,
a sentiment of good things to be conserved. It
was something dynamic and creative, seeking to build
a better and more modern nation, constantly adapted
to the development of the age and inspiring it.

—*Oswald Mosley*

This is the most magnificent movement of all! There
is a dignity, a majesty, a sublimity, in this last effort of the
patriots that I greatly admire. The people should never
rise without doing something to be remembered—
something notable and striking. This destruction of the tea
is so bold, so daring, so firm, intrepid and inflexible, and it
must have so important consequences, and so lasting, that
I can't but consider it as an epocha in history!

—*John Adams*

One country, one constitution, one destiny.

—*Daniel Webster*

I don't know much about patriotism but I know what
I like. The U.S. Constitution. I like that. The sight of
fellow citizens doing something generous and valuable
for one another. The knowledge that we belong to a
system dedicated to equal stature and equal changes. Such
things make me and most feel good about our country.

—*Roger Rosenblatt*

I venture to suggest that patriotism is not a short
and frenzied outburst of emotion but the tranquil
and steady dedication of a lifetime.

—*Adlai Stevenson*

And so, my fellow Americans: Ask not what your country
can do for you—ask what you can do for your country.

—*John F. Kennedy*

Patriotism is just loyalty to friends, people, families.

—*Robert Santos*

So to be patriots as not to forget we are gentlemen.

—*Edmund Burke*

Peace & Nonviolence

Peace is more important than all justice;
and peace was not made for the sake of justice,
but justice for the sake of peace.
—*Martin Luther*

Peace is not an absence of war, it is a virtue, a state
of mind, a disposition for benevolence, confidence, justice.
—*Benedict Spinoza*

You can't separate peace from freedom because
no one can be at peace unless he has his freedom.
—*Malcolm X*

The god of victory is said to be one-handed, but peace
gives victory on both sides.
—*Ralph Waldo Emerson*

There is no way to peace; peace is the way.
—*A. J. Muste*

Nothing good ever comes of violence.
—*Martin Luther*

Peace is a journey of a thousand miles
and it must be taken one step at a time.
—*Lyndon B. Johnson*

We should wage war not to win war, but to win peace.
—*Paul Hoffman*

If they want peace, nations should avoid
the pin-pricks that precede cannonshots.
—*Napoleon Bonaparte*

Peace is a daily, a weekly, a monthly process,
gradually changing opinions, slowly eroding
old barriers, quietly building new structures.
—*John F. Kennedy*

Blessed are the peacemakers on earth.
—*William Shakespeare*

Peace is rarely denied to the peaceful.
—*Johann von Schiller*

He is the happiest, be he king or peasant,
who finds peace in his home.
—*Johann Wolfgang von Goethe*

Nothing can bring you peace but yourself.
—*Ralph Waldo Emerson*

The structure of world peace cannot be the work
of one man, or one party, or one nation. . . . It must be a peace
which rests on the cooperative effort of the whole world.
—*Franklin D. Roosevelt*

Today the real test of power is not capacity
to make war but capacity to prevent it.
—*Anne O'Hare McCormick*

To be at peace with God and man,
that is well-being indeed.
—*Johanna Spyri*

Peace is the one condition of survival in this nuclear age.
—*Adlai Stevenson*

Beneath the rule of men entirely great,
The pen is mightier than the sword.
—*Edward Bulwer-Lytton*

Peace can endure only so long as humanity really insists
upon it, and is willing to work for it—and sacrifice for it.
—*Franklin D. Roosevelt*

Let us have peace.
—*Ulysses S. Grant*

We seek peace, knowing that peace
is the climate of freedom.
—*Dwight D. Eisenhower*

Sometime they'll give a war and nobody will come.
—*Carl Sandburg*

If we are to live in peace, we must
come to know each other better.
—*Lyndon B. Johnson*

There never was a good war or a bad peace.
—*Benjamin Franklin*

The example of American must be the example
not merely of peace because it will not fight, but
of peace because peace is the healing and elevating
influence of the world, and strife is not.
—*Woodrow Wilson*

It is best to win without fighting.
—*Sun-Tzu*

Avoid popularity if you would have peace.
—*Abraham Lincoln*

He is wise who tries everything before arms.
—*Terence*

It isn't enough to talk about peace. One must believe in it. And it isn't enough to believe in it. One must work at it.
—*Eleanor Roosevelt*

When life is so tiresome, there ain't no peace like the greatest peace—the peace of the Lord's hand holding you.
—*William H. Armstrong*

To be prepared for war is one of the most effective means of preserving peace.
—*George Washington*

Peace is not an absence of war, it is a virtue, a state of mind, a disposition for benevolence, confidence, justice.
—*Benedict Spinoza*

The ballot is stronger than the bullet.
—*Abraham Lincoln*

You may call for peace as loudly as you wish, but where there is no brotherhood there can in the end be no peace.
—*Max Lerner*

Perseverance & Persistence

Most of the important things in the world have
been accomplished by people who have kept on
trying when there seemed to be no hope at all.
—*Dale Carnegie*

Effort only fully releases its reward
after a person refuses to quit.
—*Napoleon Hill*

Energy and persistence conquer all things.
—*Benjamin Franklin*

Little minds are tamed and subdued by misfortune;
but great minds rise above them.
—*Washington Irving*

A man is not finished when he is defeated.
He is finished when he quits.
—*Richard Nixon*

Nothing in the world can take the place of persistence.
Talent will not; nothing is more common than
unsuccessful men of talent. Genius will not;
unrewarded genius is almost a proverb. Education
will not; the world is full of educated derelicts.
Persistence and determination alone are omnipotent.
—*Calvin Coolidge*

Few things are impossible to diligence and skill ... Great
works are performed, not by strength, but perseverance.
—*Samuel Johnson*

The difference between perseverance and
obstinacy is that one often comes from a strong
will and the other from a strong won't.
—*Henry Ward Beecher*

If you can force your heart and nerve and sinew
to serve your turn long after they are gone, and so
hold on when there is nothing in you except
the will which says to them: 'Hold on!'
—*Rudyard Kipling*

My definition of losing is not somebody who loses a game.
Losing is giving up . . . Everyone can be a winner in life.
—*Cheryl Miller*

Prosperity is a great teacher; adversity
is a greater. Possession pampers the mind;
privation trains and strengthens it.
—*William Hazlitt*

Consider the postage stamp: its usefulness consists in the
ability to stick to one thing till it gets there.
—*Josh Billings*

Let me tell you the secret that has led me to my goal.
My strength lies solely in my tenacity.
—*Louis Pasteur*

Out of every crisis, every tribulation, every disaster,
mankind rises with some share of greater knowledge,
of higher decency, or purer purpose.
—*Franklin D. Roosevelt*

341

I've never quite believed that one chance is all I get.
—*Anne Tyler*

It matters if you just don't give up.
—*Stephen Hawking*

Regardless of what they say about it, we are
going to keep it . . . I don't believe I ought
to quit because I am not a quitter.
—*Richard Nixon*

'Tis a lesson you should heed,
Try, try again.
—*Thomas H. Palmer*

Never give up and never face the facts.
—*Ruth Gordon*

It's always too early to quit.
—*Norman Vincent Peale*

I hope to go on and on.
—*Margaret Thatcher*

Well, back to the old drawing board.
—*Peter Arno*

He conquers who endures.
—*Persius*

Perseverance is more prevailing than violence; and many things which cannot be overcome when they are together yield themselves up when taken little by little.
—*Plutarch*

Whatever I engage in, I must push inordinately.
—*Andrew Carnegie*

Even the woodpecker woes his success to the fact that he uses his head and keeps pecking away until he finishes the job he starts.
—*Coleman Cox*

Most people give up just when they're about
to achieve success. They quit on the one yard line.
They give up at the last minute of the game one
foot from a winning touchdown.

—*H. Ross Perot*

The greatest accomplishment is not in never
falling, but in rising again after you fall.

—*Vince Lombardi*

I think, perhaps, as I look back at those who shaped
my own life—and there are a great deal of similarities
between the game of football and the game of politics—
that I learned a great deal from a football coach who
not only taught his players how to win but also taught
them that when you lose you don't quit, that when
you lose you fight harder the next time.

—*Richard Nixon*

Never let your head hang down. Never give up and
sit down and grieve. Find another way. And don't pray
when it rains if you don't pray when the sun shines.

—*Satchel Paige*

Out of the wreck I rise.
—*Robert Browning*

It isn't the mountain ahead that wears you
out—it's the grain of sand in your shoe.
—*Robert W. Service*

Although there are countless alumni of the
school of hard knocks, there has not yet been
a move to accredit that institution.
—*Sonya Rudikoff*

All happiness depends on courage and work. I have
had many periods of wretchedness, but with energy and
above all with illusions, I pulled through them all.
—*Honoré de Balzac*

I speak to the black experience, but I am always talking
about the human condition—about what we can endure,
dream, fail at, and still survive.
—*Maya Angelou*

I know of no higher fortitude than
stubbornness in the face of overwhelming odds.
—*Louis Nizer*

Whether it be to failure of success,
the first need of being is endurance—to endure
with gladness if we can, with fortitude in any event.
—*Bliss Carman*

The Saints are the Sinners who keep on trying.
—*Robert Louis Stevenson*

Fight on, my merry men all,
I'm a little wounded, but I am not slain;
I will lay me down for to bleed a while,
Then I'll rise and fight with you again.
—*John Dryden*

That which we persist in doing becomes
easier—not that the nature of the task has
changed, but our ability to do has increased.
—*Ralph Waldo Emerson*

To dry one's eyes and laugh at a fall,
And baffled, get up and begin again.
—*Robert Browning*

Push on—keep moving.
—*Thomas Morton*

We shall not flag or fail. We shall fight in France,
we shall fight on the seas and oceans, we shall fight
with growing confidence and growing strength in the air,
we shall defend our island, whatever the cost may be, we
shall fight on the beaches, we shall fight on the landing
grounds, we shall fight in the fields and in the streets, we
shall fight in the hills; we shall never surrender.
—*Winston Churchill*

Yet no matter what happens, if all these things fail,
fall completely to the ground and shatter into a million
pieces, it's not going to fundamentally affect us or
what we do. We're going to keep on playing.
—*Jerry Garcia*

Out of the earth, the rose,
Out of the night, the dawn:
Out of my heart, with all its woes,
High courage to press on.
—*Laura Lee Mitchel*

Nothing great was ever done without much enduring.
—*St. Catherine of Siena*

Well begun is half done.

—*Aristotle*

Preparation

Be Prepared . . . the meaning of the motto is that a
scout must prepare himself by previous thinking out
and practicing how to act on any accident or emergency
so that he is never taken by surprise; he knows exactly
what to do when anything unexpected happens.

—Sir Robert Baden-Powell

To penetrate one's being, one must go armed to the teeth.

—Paul Valéry

Luck is a matter of preparation meeting opportunity.

—Oprah Winfrey

Have thy tools ready. God will find thee work.

—Sir James Murray

In the field of observation,
chance favours the prepared mind.

—Louis Pasteur

We must cultivate our garden.
—Voltaire

In preparing for battle, I have always found that
plans are useless, but planning is indispensable.
—Dwight D. Eisenhower

Chance favors the prepared mind.
—Louis Pasteur

The art of living is more like that of wrestling
than of dancing. The main thing is to stand firm
and be ready for an unforeseen attack.
—Marcus Aurelius Antoninus

You'll find us rough, sir, but you'll find us ready.
—Charles Dickens

Reason

Reason is God's crowning gift to man.

—*Sophocles*

I'll not listen to reason. . . . Reason always
means what someone else has got to say.

—*Elizabeth Cleghorn Gaskell*

Reason is man's faculty for grasping the world
by thought, in contradiction to intelligence, which
is man's ability to manipulate the world with the help
of thought. Reason is man's instrument for arriving at
the truth, intelligence is man's instrument for manipulating
the world more successfully; the former is essentially
human, the latter belongs to the animal part of man.

—*Erich Fromm*

Reason over passion.

—*Pierre Elliott Trudeau*

Reason is also choice.

—*John Milton*

To see what is in front of one's
nose needs a constant struggle.
—*George Orwell*

"Contrariwise," continued Tweedledee,
"if it was so, it might be; and if it were so,
it would be, but as it isn't, it ain't. That's logic."
—*Lewis Carroll*

If well thou hast begun, go on;
it is the end that crowns us, not the fight.
—*Robert Herrick*

A life based on reason will always require to be
balanced by an occasional bout of violent and irrational
emotion, for the instinctual tribes must be satisfied.
—*Cyril Connolly*

The sign of an intelligent people is their ability
to control emotions by the application of reason.
—*Marya Mannes*

Relationships

May the gods grant you all things which your heart
desires, and may they give you a husband and a home
and gracious concord, for there is nothing greater
and better than this -when a husband and wife keep
a household in oneness of mind, a great woe to their
enemies and joy to their friends, and win high renown.
—*Homer*

All for one, one for all, that is our motto.
—*Alexandre Dumas the Elder*

Every man who is high up loves to think that he has done
it all himself, and the wife smiles, and lets it go at that.
—*James Matthew Barrie*

The same heart beats in every human breast.
—*Matthew Arnold*

Marriage is our last, best chance to grow up.
—*Joseph Barth*

Our chief want in life is somebody
who shall make us do what we can.
—*Ralph Waldo Emerson*

If men and women are to understand each other,
to enter into each other's nature with mutual sympathy,
and to become capable of genuine comradeship,
the foundation must be laid in youth.
—*Havelock Ellis*

Most men who are not married by the age
of thirty-five are either homosexual or really smart.
—*Becky Rodenbeck*

The family that prays together stays together.
—*Al Scalpone*

I've had the boyhood thing of being Elvis.
Now I want to be with my best friend, and my best
friend's my wife. Who could ask for anything more?
—*John Lennon*

I married the first man I ever kissed. When
I tell my children that they just about throw up.
—*Barbara Bush*

Men's hearts ought not to be set against one another,
but set with one another, and all against evil only.
—*Thomas Carlyle*

The sexes were made for each other, and only
in the wise and loving union of the two is the fullness
of health and duty and happiness to be expected.
—*William Hall*

In the field of world policy, I would dedicate
this nation to the policy of the good neighbor.
—*Franklin D. Roosevelt*

If you treat men the way they are you never improve them.
If you treat them the way you want them to be, you do.
—*Johann Wolfgang von Goethe*

Other men are lenses through
which we read our own minds.
—*François de la Rochefoucauld*

Let us at all times remember that all American
citizens are brothers of a common country, and
should dwell together in bonds of fraternal feeling.
—*Abraham Lincoln*

There are no problems we cannot solve together,
and very few that we can solve by ourselves.
—*Lyndon B. Johnson*

Marriage has many pains, but celibacy has no pleasures.
—*Samuel Johnson*

Some people are your relatives but others are your
ancestors, and you choose the ones you want to have
as ancestors. You create yourself out of those values.
—*Ralph Ellison*

Marriage is not just spiritual communion and
passionate embraces; marriage is also three-meals-a-day
and remembering to take out the trash.

—Joyce Brothers

You get the best out of others when
you give the best of yourself.

—Harry Firestone

Blessed is the influence of one true,
loving human soul on another.

—George Eliot

The dear little wife at home, John,
With ever so much to do,
Stitches to set and babies to pet,
And so many thoughts of you—
The beautiful household fairy,
Filling your heart with light—
Whatever you meet today, John,
Go cheerily home tonight.

—Mary Lowe Dickinson

If you don't understand yourself you
don't understand anybody else.
—*Nikki Giovanni*

There is no such thing as Society. There are individual
men and women, and there are families. And no government can do anything except through people, and people
must look to themselves first. It's our duty to look
after ourselves and then to look after our neighbour.
—*Margaret Thatcher*

The important thing is not what they
think of me, it is what I think of them.
—*Victoria, Queen of England*

The formula for achieving a successful relationship is
simple: you should treat all disasters as if they were
trivialities but never treat a triviality as if it were a disaster.
—*Quentin Crisp*

On this sunken globe, men can no longer live as strangers.
—*Adlai Stevenson*

We make our friends; we make our enemies;
but God makes our next-door neighbor.
—*G. K. Chesterton*

A loving person lives in a loving world. A hostile person
lives in a hostile world: everyone you meet is your mirror.
—*Ken Keyes, Jr.*

Make yourself necessary to somebody.
—*Ralph Waldo Emerson*

I am a part of all that I have met.
—*Lord Tennyson*

It is well to remember that the entire population of the
universe, with one trifling exception, is composed of others.
—*John Andrew Holmes*

Marriage is the deep, deep peace of the double
bed after the hurly-burly of the chaise longue.
—*Mrs. Patrick Campbell*

A wise woman will always let her husband have her way.
—*Richard Brinsley Sheridan*

I love men, not because they are men,
but because they are not women.
—*Christina, Queen of Sweden*

A good marriage is that in which each appoints the other guardian of his solitude. Once the realization is accepted that even between the closest human beings infinite distances continue to exist, a wonderful living side by side can grow up, if they succeed in loving the distance between them which makes it possible for each to see the other whole and against a side sky.
—*Rainer Maria Rilke*

Rewards

The reward of a thing well done, is to have done it.
—*Ralph Waldo Emerson*

The applause of a single human
being is of great consequence.
—*Samuel Johnson*

These are the times that try men's souls. The summer
soldier and the sunshine patriot will, in this crisis, shrink
from the service of their country, but he that stands it
now, deserves the love and thanks of man and woman.
Tyranny, like hell, is not easily conquered; yet we have
this consolation with us, that the harder the conflict,
the more glorious the triumph.
—*Thomas Paine*

We cannot make events. Our business is wisely
to improve them. . . . Mankind are governed more
by their feelings than by reason. Events which excite
those feelings will produce wonderful effects.
—*Samuel Adams*

The end of labor is to gain leisure.

—*Aristotle*

Not-really-trying is just as much effort as
trying-really-hard. The only difference . . .
is that not-really-trying receives no reward.

—*A. N. Wilson*

The effects of our actions may be postponed but they
are never lost. There is an inevitable reward for good deeds
and an inescapable punishment for bad. Meditate upon this
truth, and seek always to earn good wages from Destiny.

—*Wu Ming Fu*

Whatever our creed, we feel that no good deed can
by any possibility go unrewarded, no evil deed unpunished.

—*Orison S. Marden*

No man, who continues to add something to the
material, intellectual and moral well-being of the place
in which he lives, is left long without proper reward.

—*Booker T. Washington*

The reward for work well done
is the opportunity to do more.

—*Jonas Salk*

Let the motive be in the deed and not in the event.
Be not one whose motive for action is the hope of reward.

—*Johnas Kreeshna Salk*

The reward of one duty is the power to fulfill another.

—*George Eliot*

Simple this tale!—but delicately perfumed
As the sweet roadside honeysuckle. That's why,
Difficult though its meter was to tackle,
I'm glad I wrote it.

—*Sir Arthur Quiller-Couch*

The whole of what we know is a system
of compensations. Each suffering is rewarded;
each sacrifice is made up; every debt is paid.

—*Ralph Waldo Emerson*

No person was ever honoured for what he received.
Honour has been the reward for what he gave.
—*Calvin Coolidge*

For those who are willing to make an effort,
great miracles and wonderful treasures are in store.
—*Isaac Bashevis Singer*

For the wages of sin is death, but the free gift
of God is eternal life in Christ Jesus our Lord.
—*adapted from Romans 6:23*

The only reward of virtue is virtue.
—*Ralph Waldo Emerson*

No gains without pains.
—*Adlai Stevenson*

A favor well bestowed is almost as great an honor
to him who confers it as to him who receives it.
—*Sir Richard Steele*

Self-Esteem & Confidence

Insist on yourself; never imitate. Your own gift
you can present every moment with the cumulative
force of a whole life's cultivation; but of the adopted talent
of another you have only an extemporaneous half possession. . . . Do that which is assigned to you, and you
cannot hope too much or dare too much.

—*Ralph Waldo Emerson*

I have another duty equally sacred . . . My duty to myself.

—*Henrik Ibsen*

No man should think himself a zero, and think
he can do nothing about the state of the world.

—*Bernard Baruch*

The history of the world is full of men who rose to leadership, by sheer force of self-confidence, bravery and tenacity.

—*Gandhi*

They are able who think they are able.

—*Virgil*

365

Oftentimes nothing profits more than
self-esteem, grounded on what is just and right.
—*John Milton*

Calm self-confidence is as far from conceit as the
desire to earn a decent living is remote from greed.
—*Channing Pollock*

There is no indispensable man.
—*Franklin D. Roosevelt*

The worst loneliness is not
to be comfortable with yourself.
—*Mark Twain*

I am as my Creator made me, and since
He is satisfied, so am I.
—*Minnie Smith*

For they conquer who believe they can.
—*John Dryden*

You can be pleased with nothing
when you are not pleased with yourself.
—*Mary Wortley Montagu*

If it's me against 48, I feel sorry for the 48.
—*Margaret Thatcher*

You must believe in yourself, my son, or
no one else will believe in you. Be self-confident,
self-reliant, and even if you don't make it, you will
know you have done your best. Now, go to it.
—*Mary Hardy MacArthur*

To be nobody but yourself—in a world which is doing
its best, night and day, to make you everybody else—
means to fight the hardest battle which any human
being can fight, and never stop fighting.
—*e. e. cummings*

It is necessary to the happiness of a man
that he be mentally faithful to himself.
—*Thomas Paine*

True prosperity is the result of well-placed
confidence in ourselves and our fellow man.
—*Benjamin Burt*

If you can't get a compliment
any other way, pay yourself one.
—*Mark Twain*

Have confidence that if you have done a little
thing well, you can do a bigger thing well, too.
—*David Storey*

Never violate the sacredness of your individual self-respect.
—*Theodore Parker*

The feeling of accomplishment welled up inside of me . . .
three Olympic gold medals. I knew that was something
nobody could ever take away from me, ever.
—*Wilma Rudolph*

Don't compromise yourself. You are all you've got.
—*Janis Joplin*

Be thy own palace, or the world's thy jail.
—*John Donne*

Humility is no substitute for a good personality.
—*Fran Lebowitz*

For a man to achieve all that is demanded of him
he must regard himself as greater than he is.
—*Johann Wolfgang von Goethe*

If I am not for myself, who will be?
—*Pirke Avot*

I have entered on an enterprise which is without
precedent, and will have no imitator. I propose to
show my fellows a man as nature made him, and
this man shall be myself.
—*Jean-Jacques Rousseau*

The greatest success is successful self-acceptance.
—*Ben Sweet*

Be yourself. Who else is better qualified?
—Frank J. Giblin

Self-confidence is the first requisite to great undertakings.
—Samuel Johnson

I have never seen a greater monster
or miracle in the world than myself.
—Michel E. de Montaigne

We are all worms, but I do believe that I am a glow-worm.
—Winston Churchill

Compassion for myself is the
most powerful healer of them all.
—Theodore Isaac Rubin

Persons of high self-esteem are not driven to make
themselves superior to others. . . . Their joy is being
who they are, not in being better than someone else.
—Nathaniel Branden

A man cannot be comfortable without his own approval.
—*Mark Twain*

I owe my fame only to myself.
—*Pierre Corneille*

I am more afraid of my own heart than of the Pope and all his cardinals. I have within me the great Pope, Self.
—*Martin Luther*

I share no man's opinions; I have my own.
—*Ivan Sergeyevich Turgenev*

I'm the greatest!
—*Muhammad Ali*

Nobody knows what's in him until he tries to pull it out.
—*Ernest Hemingway*

I would rather be right than be President.
—*Henry Clay*

His brow is wet with honest sweat,
He earns whate'er he can,
And looks the whole world in the face,
For he owes not any man.
—*Henry Wadsworth Longfellow*

I am a Shawnee. My forefathers were warriors. Their son is a warrior. From them I take only my existence. From my tribe I take nothing. I am the maker of my own fortune. And oh, that I might make the fortunes of my red people, and of my country, as great as the conceptions of my mind, when I think of the Great Spirit that rules this universe.
—*Tecumseh*

Every man paddle his own canoe.
—*Frederick Marryat*

Silence & Brevity

Well-timed silence hath more eloquence than speech.
—Martin Farquhar Tupper

Do not the most moving moments
of our lives find us all without words?
—Marcel Marceau

Drawing on my fine command
of the English language, I said nothing.
—Robert Benchley

My personal hobbies are reading,
listening to music, and silence.
—Edith Sitwell

Never express yourself more
clearly than you are able to think.
—Niels Bohr

Silence is the ultimate weapon of power.
—*Charles de Gaulle*

There is danger when a man throws his tongue
into high gear before he gets his brain a-going.
—*C. C. Phelps*

I wish people who have trouble
communicating would just shut up.
—*Tom Lehrer*

Women like silent men. They think they're listening.
—*Marcel Archard*

Speech is the small change of silence.
—*George Meredith*

If you would be pungent, be brief; for
it is with words as with sunbeams—the more
they are condensed, the deeper they burn.
—*Robert Southey*

The good and the wise lead quiet lives.
—*Euripides*

Silence is one of the hardest arguments to refute.
—*Josh Billings*

Seal up your lips and give no words but mum.
—*William Shakespeare*

The more you say, the less people remember.
The fewer the words, the greater the profit.
—*Fénelon*

If you keep your mouth shut you
will never put your foot in it.
—*Austin O'Malley*

While with an eye made quiet by the power
Of harmony, and the deep power of joy,
We see into the life of things.
—*William Wordsworth*

Brevity is the best recommendation of speech,
whether in a senator or an orator.
—*Marcus Tullius Cicero*

———•———

To have a quiet mind is to possess one's mind wholly;
to have a calm spirit is to possess one's self.
—*Hamilton Mabie*

———•———

Speech was given to the ordinary sort of men
whereby to communicate their mind; but
to wise men, whereby to conceal it.
—*Robert South*

———•———

All the great pleasures in life are silent.
—*Georges Clemenceau*

———•———

Silence is golden.
—*Thomas Carlyle*

———•———

One of the best ways to persuade others is with your ears.
—*Dean Rusk*

Speak low, speak slow, and don't say much.
—*John Wayne*

Noise proves nothing. Often a hen who has merely
laid an egg cackles as if she had laid an asteroid.
—*Mark Twain*

The fair request ought to be
followed by the deed, in silence.
—*Dante Alighieri*

The fewer the words, the better the prayer.
—*Martin Luther*

Go placidly amid the noise and the haste,
and remember what peace there may be in silence.
—*Max Ehrmann*

You must learn to be still in the midst
of activity and to be vibrantly alive in repose.
—*Indira Gandhi*

We need a reason to speak, but none to keep silent.
—*Pierre Nicole*

Brevity is a great charm of eloquence.
—*Marcus Tullius Cicero*

That man's silence is wonderful to listen to.
—*Thomas Hardy*

He has the gift of quiet.
—*John Le Carré*

Let a fool hold his tongue and he will pass for a sage.
—*Publilius Syrus*

Think before thou speakest.
—*Miguel de Cervantes*

The harvest of a quiet eye.
—*William Wordsworth*

Never say more than is necessary.
—*Richard Brinsley Sheridan*

Blessed is the man who, having nothing to say,
abstains from giving in words evidence of the fact.
—*George Eliot*

People who know little are usually great talkers,
while men who know much say little.
—*Jean-Jacques Rousseau*

What physic, what chirurgery, what wealth, favor,
authority can relieve, bear out, assuage, or expel
a troubled conscience? A quiet mind cureth all.
—*Robert Burton*

The greatest triumphs of propaganda have been
accomplished, not by doing something, but by
refraining from doing. Great is truth, but still greater,
from a practical point of view, is silence about truth.
—*Aldous Huxley*

Strongest minds
Are often those of whom the noisy world
Hears least.
—*William Wordsworth*

Silence is deep as Eternity; speech, shallow as Time.
—*Thomas Carlyle*

The most silent people are generally those
who think most highly of themselves.
—*William Hazlitt*

Create, artist! Do not talk!
—*Johann Wolfgang von Goethe*

Nature has given to men one tongue, but two ears,
that we may hear from others twice as much as we speak.
—*Epictetus*

I have noticed that nothing
I never said ever did me any harm.
—*Calvin Coolidge*

Simple Pleasures

Our life is frittered away by detail.... Simplify, simplify.
—*Henry David Thoreau*

Very little is needed to make a happy life.
—*Marcus Aurelius Antoninus*

Less is more.

—*Robert Browning*

He does not seem to me to be a free man
who does not sometimes do nothing.
—*Marcus Tullius Cicero*

Give me books, fruit, French wine and fine weather and a
little music out of doors, played by someone I do not know.
—*John Keats*

And all the loveliest things there be
Come simply, so it seems to me.
—*Edna St. Vincent Millay*

Live in each season as it passes . . . breathe
the air, drink the drink, taste the fruit.
—*Henry David Thoreau*

To make pleasures pleasant, shorten them.
—*Charles Buxton*

Women have simple tastes. Thy get pleasure out of
the conversation of children in arms and men in love.
—*H. L. Mencken*

My advice to you is not to inquire why
or whither, but just enjoy your ice cream while
it's on your plate—that's my philosophy.
—*Thornton Wilder*

I have learned to have very modest goals
for society and myself, things like clean air,
green grass, children with bright eyes, not being
pushed around, usefull work that suit's one's abilities,
plain tasty food, and occasional satisfying nookie.
—*Paul Goodman*

It is the small, insignificant, simple gestures that make life
bearable. A smile, a touch, a word, a kindness, a concern.
—*Pam Brown*

Why is life worth living? That's a very good question.
Ummm . . . Well there are certain things, I guess, that
make it worthwhile. Uh, like what? Okay. Um, for
me . . . oh, I would say . . . what, Groucho Marx,
to name one thing and . . . Willie Mays, and . . . the
second movement of the *Jupiter Symphony,*
and . . . Louis Armstrong's recording of "Potato Head
Blues" . . . Swedish movies, naturally . . . Sentimental
Education by Flaubert . . . and Marlon Brando, Frank
Sinatra . . . those incredible apples and pears by Cezanne.
—*Woody Allen*

We act as though comfort and luxury were the chief
repuirements of life, when all that we need to make
us really happy is something to be enthusiastic about.
—*Charles Kingsley*

Let us have wine and women, mirth and laughter,
Sermons and soda-water the day after.
—*Lord Byron*

If you resolve to give up smoking, drinking and loving,
you don't actually live longer; it just seems longer.
—*Clement Freud*

Basically, I'm interested in friendship, sex and death.
—*Sharon Riis*

When I was very young, I kissed my first woman, and
smoked my first cigarette on the same day. Believe me,
never since have I wasted any more time on tobacco.
—*Arturo Toscanini*

There is nothing like staying at home for real comfort.
—*Jane Austen*

One's first book, kiss, home run is always the best.
—*Clifton Fadiman*

Out of intense complexities, intense simplicities emerge.
—*Winston Churchill*

We ascribe beauty to that which is simple; which has no
superfluous parts; which exactly answers its ends.
—*Ralph Waldo Emerson*

Leisure is being allowed to do nothing.
—*G. K. Chesterton*

Most of the luxuries, and many of the so-called
comforts, of life are not only not indispensable,
but positive hindrances to the elevation of mankind.
—*Henry David Thoreau*

When the voices of children are heard on the green
And laughing is heard on the hill,
My heart is a rest within my breast
And everything is still.
—*William Blake*

Until I saw Chardin's painting, I never realized how much
beauty lay around me in my parents' house, in the half-
cleared table, in the corner of a tablecloth left awry, in the
knife beside the empty oyster shell.
—*Marcel Proust*

To own a bit of ground, to scratch it with a hoe,
to plant seeds, and watch the renewal of life—this is the
commonest delight of the race, the most satisfactory thing
a man can do.
—*Charles Dudley Warner*

It is so small a thing
To have enjoyed the sun,
To have lived light in the spring,
To have loved, to have thought, to have done.
—*Matthew Arnold*

One ought, every day at least, to hear a little song,
read a good poem, see a fine picture, and, if it were
possible, to speak a few reasonable words.
—*Johann Wolfgang von Goethe*

Success

A first failure may prepare the way for later success.
—Arnold Lobel

The first and most important step toward ...
success is the feeling that we can succeed.
—Nelson Boswell

There is a passion for perfection which you will
rarely see fully developed; but you may note this fact,
that in successful lives it is never wholly lacking.
—Bliss Carman

When men drink, then they are rich and
successful and win lawsuits and are happy and help
their friends. Quickly, bring me a beaker of wine, so
that I may wet my mind and say something clever.
—Aristophanes

Man is not made for defeat.
—Ernest Hemingway

I don't know the key to success, but the key
to failure is trying to please everybody.
—*Bill Cosby*

As a general rule the most successful man
in life is the man who has the best information.
—*Benjamin Disraeli*

To succeed in the world, you must also be well-mannered.
—*Voltaire*

Experience shows that success is due less
to ability than to zeal. The winner is he who
gives himself to his work, body and soul.
—*Charles Buxton*

Part of the secret of success in life is to eat
what you like and let the food fight it out inside.
—*Mark Twain*

The successful people are the ones who can think
up things for the rest of the world to keep busy at.
—*Don Marquis*

We are not interested in the possibilities of defeat.
They do not exist here.
—*Victoria, Queen of England*

The men who succeed are the efficient few.
They are the few who have the ambition
and willpower to develop themselves.
—*Herbert N. Casson*

Not only have women been successful in entering fields
in which men are supposed to have a more natural
aptitude, but they have created entirely new businesses.
—*Lucretia P. Hunter*

Failure? Do you remember what Queen Victoria
once said? "Failure?—the possibilities do not exist."
—*Margaret Thatcher*

Life affords no higher pleasure than that of surmounting
difficulties, passing from one step of success to another,
forming new wishes and seeing them gratified.
—*Samuel Johnson*

It is a deep-seated belief on the part of almost
all Americans that their success will be better assured
as they help to build the success of others.
—*Paul Hoffman*

When a man succeeds, he does it in spite of everybody,
and not with the assistance of everybody.
—*Edgar Watson Howe*

I used to live in a sewer. Now I live in a swamp.
I've come up in the world.
—*Linda Darnell*

Any fact facing us is not as important as our attitude
toward it, for that determines our success or failure.
The way you think about a fact may defeat you before
you ever do anything about it. You are overcome by
the fact because you think you are.
—*Norman Vincent Peale*

Sometimes it's worse to win a fight than to lose.
—*Billie Holiday*

The toughest thing about success
is that you've got to keep on being a success.
—*Irving Berlin*

Successful people never fail, because
they turn their failures into wisdom.
—*Jim and Charles Fay*

Success has never been a part of our schedule,
exactly. It's kind of been a happy surprise.
—*Jerry Garcia*

A man's homeland is wherever he prospers.
—*Aristophanes*

Success is the progressive realization of a worthy ideal.
—*Earl Nightingale*

There is only one success—to be able
to spend your life in your own way.
—*Christopher Morley*

Success is not the result of spontaneous combustion.
You must set yourself on fire.
—*Reggie Leach*

Success is like a vitamin. If you don't get enough
of it growing up, you'll suffer a very severe deficiency
that could have long-term impacts in your life.
—*Mel Levine*

God doesn't require that we succeed;
he only requires that you try.
—*Mother Teresa*

How can they say my life isn't a success?
Have I not for more than sixty years got
enough to eat and escaped being eaten?
—*Logan Pearsall Smith*

Success is that old A B C—ability, breaks and courage.
—*Charles Luckman*

Success is having ten honeydew melons
and eating only the top half of each one.
—*Barbra Streisand*

Success is more a function of consistent
common sense than it is of genius.
—*Al Wang*

Let's not forget James Brown picked cotton.
James Brown shined shoes. And yet James Brown
is still active. Because James Brown worked all the
way to the top. . . . I first started out tryin' to get a decent
meal, a decent pair of shoes, so when I got to where I
could do that, I thought I was on the top anyway.

—*James Brown*

Of course there is no formula for success except perhaps,
an unconditional acceptance of life and what it brings.

—*Artur Rubinstein*

You always pass failure on the way to success.

—*Mickey Rooney*

A great secret of success is to go through
life as a man who never gets used up.

—*Albert Schweitzer*

All success consists in this: You are doing something
for somebody—benefiting humanity—and the feeling
of success comes from the consciousness of this.

—*Elbert Hubbard*

Real success is to know that you helped
others to change their lives for the better.
—*Dan Sosa, Jr.*

A minute's success pays the failure of years.
—*Robert Browning*

Behind every successful man
there's a lot of unsuccessful years.
—*Bob Brown*

There are few successful adults who
were not first successful children.
—*Alexander Chase*

I stopped believing in Santa Claus when I was six.
Mother took me to see him in a department store
and he asked for my autograph.
—*Shirley Temple*

The secret of success is constancy to purpose.
—*Benjamin Disraeli*

I must admit that I personally measure success
in terms of the contributions an individual makes
to her or his fellow human beings.
—*Margaret Mead*

I have learned that success is to be measured not so much
by the position that one has reached in life as by the
obstacles which he has overcome while trying to succeed.
—*Booker T. Washington*

The way to success: First have a clear goal, not a fuzzy
one. Sharpen this goal until it becomes specific and
clearly defined in your conscious mind. Hold it there
until, by a process of spiritual and intellectual osmosis . . .
it seeps into your unconscious. Then you will have it
because it has you. Surround this goal constantly with
positive thoughts and faith. Give it positive follow-through.
That is the way success is achieved.
—*Norman Vincent Peale*

You have to want it [success] bad. You can find
geniuses on any skid row and average intellects as
presidents of banks. It's what pushes you from inside.
—*Charley Winner*

An example from the monkey: The higher
it climbs the more you see of its behind.
—*St. Bonaventure*

———•———

We can only do the best we can with what we have.
That, after all, is the measure of success.
—*Marguerite de Angeli*

———•———

The men who try to do something and fail are infinitely
better than those who try to do nothing and succeed.
—*Lloyd Jones*

———•———

My recipe for success is hard work,
patience, honesty, and total commitment.
—*Dave Thomas*

———•———

It takes time to win success.

—*Aesop*

———•———

Eighty percent of success is showing up.
—*Woody Allen*

What is success?
To laugh often and much;
to win the respect of intelligent people
and the affection of children;
to earn the appreciation of honest critics
and to endure the betrayal of false friends;
to appreciate beauty;
to find the best in others;
to leave the world a bit better whether by a healthy child,
a garden patch or a redeemed social condition;
to know even one life has breathed easier because you
have lived.
This is to have succeeded.
—*Ralph Waldo Emerson*

Taking Action

Be always sure you're right—then go ahead.
—David Crockett

———•———

He started to sing as he tackled the thing
that couldn't be done, and he did it.
—Lynn Willard

———•———

If your ship doesn't come in, swim out to it!
—Jonathan Winters

———•———

Think like a man of action and
act like a man of thought.
—Henri Bergson

———•———

Men must be decided on what they will not do, and then
they are able to act with vigor in what they ought to do.
—Mencius

———•———

Go to it!

—Herbert Morrison

What you do speaks so loudly that
I cannot hear what you say.
—*Ralph Waldo Emerson*

Zeal is a volcano, the peak of which the
grass of indecisiveness does not grow.
—*Kahlil Gibran*

This Nation asks for action, and action now.
—*Franklin D. Roosevelt*

The question is: Who will get to heaven first
—the man who talks or the man who acts?
—*Melvin B. Tolson*

I am not built for academic writings.
Action is my domain.
—*Gandhi*

The great end of life is not knowledge, but action.
—*Thomas Fuller*

Ideas won't keep: something must be done about them.
—*Alfred North Whitehead*

We know what a person thinks not when he
tells us what he thinks, but by his actions.
—*Isaac Bashevis Singer*

From the moment of birth we are immersed in action,
and can only fitfully guide it by taking thought.
—*Alfred North Whitehead*

Knowing is not enough; we must apply.
Willing is not enough; we must do.
—*Johann Wolfgang von Goethe*

Every man is potentially hero and genius;
only inertia keeps men mediocre.
—*Novalis*

Procrastination is the thief of time.
—*Edward Young*

Words are not of any great importance in times of
economic disturbance. It is action that counts.
—*Herbert Hoover*

The biggest sin is sitting on your ass.
—*Florynce R. Kennedy*

I know that every good and excellent thing in
the world stands moment by moment on the
razor-edge of danger and must be fought for...
—*Thornton Wilder*

The actions of men are the best
interpreters of their thoughts.
—*John Locke*

Thought is the blossom; language
the bud; action the fruit behind it.
—*Ralph Waldo Emerson*

It is much easier to do and die than it is to reason why.
—*G. A. Studdert-Kennedy*

Action may not always bring happiness;
but there is no happiness without action.
—*Benjamin Disraeli*

It is by acts and not ideas that people live.
—*Anatole France*

Saying is one thing and doing is another.
—*Michel E. de Montaigne*

He who hesitates misses the green light, gets
bumped in the rear, and loses his parking place.
—*Herbert V. Prochnow*

One thing you should know about tears: They're
utterly useless. No point in weeping. . . . We need
to get busy and do something.
—*Lloyd Alexander*

The first blow is half the battle.
—*Oliver Goldsmith*

Action is eloquence.
—*William Shakespeare*

Long is the road from conception to completion.
—*Molière*

I came, I saw, I conquered.
—*Julius Caesar*

Do something. Do anything. But don't just
stand there and let people beat on you
and then thank them for doing it.
—*Vera and Bill Cleaver*

One must be something to be able to do something.
—*Johann Wolfgang von Goethe*

It won't do you a bit of good to know everything
if you don't do something about it.
—*Louise Fitzhugh*

To strive, to seek, to find, and not to yield.
—Lord Tennyson

Beware of rashness, but with energy and sleep
less vigilance go forward and give us victories.
—Abraham Lincoln

Thought and theory must precede all salutary action; yet
action is nobler in itself than either thought or theory.
—William Wadsworth

Well done is better than well said.
—Benjamin Franklin

Action to be effective must be directed
to clearly conceived ends.
—Jawaharlal Nehru

Instead of . . . griping, get in there
and make things better.
—George H. W. Bush

First say to yourself what you would be;
and then do what you have to do.

—*Epictetus*

The will to do, the soul to dare.

—*Sir Walter Scott*

Determine that the thing can and shall be done,
and then we shall find the way.

—*Abraham Lincoln*

For of all sad words of tongue or pen,
The saddest are these: "It might have been!"

—*John Greenleaf Whittier*

It is better to wear out than to rust out.

—*Richard Cumberland*

First ponder, then dare.

—*Helmuth von Moltke*

Indolence is a delightful but distressing state;
we must be doing something to be happy.
Action is no less necessary than thought to the
instinctive tendencies of the human frame.

—Gandhi

Sink or swim.

—William Shakespeare

You can't cross the sea merely
by standing and staring at the water.

—Rabindranath Tagore

Whatever you do, or dream you can, begin it.

—Johann Wolfgang von Goethe

I'd rather be a could-be if I cannot be an are; because
a could-be is a maybe who is reaching for a star.
I'd rather be a has-been than a might-have-been,
by far; for a might have-been has never been,
but a has was once an are.

—Milton Berle

Our main business is not to see what lies dimly in the
distance but to do what lies clearly at hand.
—*Thomas Carlyle*

We live in a wonderful world that is full of beauty,
charm and adventure. There is no end to the adventures
that we can have if only we seek them with our eyes open.
—*Jawaharlal Nehru*

I slept and dreamed that life was beauty.
I woke—and found that life was duty.
—*Ellen Sturgis Hooper*

Taking Chances & Taking Risks

The most alive is the wildest.
—Henry David Thoreau

Who dares nothing, need hope for nothing.
—Johann von Schiller

A = r + p (or Adventure equals risk plus purpose.)
—Robert McClure

One doesn't discover new lands without consenting
to lose sight of the shore for a very long time.
—André Gide

We triumph without glory when
we conquer without danger.
—Pierre Corneille

Without adventure civilization is in full decay.
—Alfred North Whitehead

When you cannot make up your mind which
of two evenly balanced courses of action you
should take—choose the bolder.

—*W. J. Slim*

The guy who takes a chance, who walks
the line between the known and unknown,
who is unafraid of failure, will succeed.

—*Gordon Parks*

You can have something that lasts throughout
your life as adventures, the times you took chances.
I think that's essential in anybody's life.

—*Jerry Garcia*

Risk! Risk anything! Care no more for the
opinions of others, for those voices. Do the hardest
thing on earth for you. Act for yourself. Face the truth.

— *Katherine Mansfield*

What you risk reveals what you value.

—*Jeanette Winterson*

Security is mostly a superstition. It does not exist in nature,
nor do the children of men as a whole experience it.
Avoiding danger is no safer in the long run than outright
exposure. Life is either a daring adventure, or nothing.
—*Helen Keller*

Behold the turtle. He makes progress
only when he sticks his neck out.
—*James Bryant Conant*

One hour of life, crowded to the full with
glorious action, and filled with noble risks, is worth
whole years of those mean observances of paltry decorum.
—*Sir Walter Scott*

Those who misrepresent the normal
experiences of life, who decry being controversial,
who shun risk, are the enemies of the American way
of life, whatever the piety of their vocal professions
and the patriotic flavor of their platitudes.
—*Henry M. Wriston*

"Why not" is a slogan for an interesting life.
—*Mason Cooley*

Two roads diverged in a wood and I—
I took the one less traveled by,
And that has made all the difference.
—*Robert Frost*

You've got to keep fighting—you've got
to risk your life every six months to stay alive.
—*Elia Kazan*

Oliver Twist has asked for more!
—*Charles Dickens*

Enter these enchanted woods,
You who dare.
—*George Meredith*

Twenty years from now you will be more
disappointed by the things you didn't do than by
the ones you did do. So throw off the bowlines.
Sail away from the safe harbor. Catch the trade
winds in your sails. Explore. Dream. Discover.
—*Mark Twain*

That is to say, anybody who can imagine themselves
doing something better than what they're doing should
just go ahead and do it, and have no fear of failure or
success but just go for it. That's all we've done.

—*Jerry Garcia*

If one is forever cautious, can one remain a human being?

—*Aleksandr Solzhenitsyn*

In skating over thin ice our safety is in our speed.

—*Ralph Waldo Emerson*

There are risks and costs to a program of action.
But they are far less than the long-range risks
and costs of comfortable inaction.

—*John F. Kennedy*

When I found I had crossed that line, I looked
at my hands to see if I was the same person.
There was such a glory over everything.

—*Harriet Tubman*

You may be disappointed if you fail,
but you are doomed if you don't try.
—*Beverly Sills*

———•———

He that leaveth nothing to Chance will do few
things ill, but he will do very few things.
—*Lord Halifax*

———•———

Only those who dare to fail
greatly can ever achieve greatly.
—*Robert F. Kennedy*

———•———

Nought venture nought have.
—*John Heywood*

———•———

Never say "no" to adventures. Always say "yes,"
otherwise you'll lead a very dull life.
—*Ian Fleming*

———•———

Great deeds are usually wrought at great risks.
—*Herodotus*

To conquer without risk is to triumph without glory.
—*Pierre Corneille*

Life is either a daring adventure or nothing.
—*Helen Keller*

Do not follow where the path may lead.
Go instead where there is no path and leave a trail.
—*Ralph Waldo Emerson*

You must do the thing you think you cannot do.
—*Eleanor Roosevelt*

One hundred percent of the shots
you don't take don't go in.
—*Wayne Gretzky*

I can accept failure. Everyone fails
at something. But I can't accept not trying.
—*Michael Jordan*

It's amazing what ordinary people can do
if they set out without preconceived notions.
—*Charles F. Kettering*

Far better is it to dare mighty things, to win
glorious triumphs, even though checkered by failure . . .
than to rank with those poor spirits who neither enjoy
much nor suffer much, because they live in a gray
twilight that knows not victory nor defeat.
—*Theodore Roosevelt*

Only those who will risk going too far
can possibly find out how far one can go.
—*T. S. Eliot*

Taking Charge & Taking Control

We must scrunch or be scrunched.
—*Charles Dickens*

Things which matter most must never be
at the mercy of things which matter least.
—*Johann Wolfgang von Goethe*

Be the change you wish to see in the world.
—*Gandhi*

If it is to be
It is up to me.
—*William H. Johnson*

Never let the other fellow set the agenda.
—*James Baker*

He will either find a way, or make one.
—*Hannibal*

Do not go gentle into that good night.
—*Dylan Thomas*

Float like a butterfly, sting like a bee.
—*Muhammad Ali*

We who lived in concentration camps can remember the men who walked through the huts comforting others, giving away their last piece of bread. They may have been few in number, but they offer sufficient proof that everything can be taken from a man but one thing: the last of human freedoms—to choose one's attitude in any given set of circumstances—to choose one's own way.
—*Viktor Frankl*

I hit big or I miss big. I like to live as big as I am.
—*George Herman "Babe" Ruth*

Time

Time is a kindly god.

—*Sophocles*

Time removes distress.

—*Terence*

Mere longevity is a good thing for those who watch Life from the sidelines. For those who play the game, an hour may be a year, a single day's work an achievement for eternity.

—*Gabriel Heatter*

The time to repair the roof is when the sun is shining.

—*John F. Kennedy*

Ideas move fast when their time comes.

—*Carolyn Heilbrun*

Carpe diem, quam minimum credula postero.
(Seize the day, put no trust in tomorrow.)

—*Horace*

The beginning is always today.
—*Mary Wollstonecraft Shelley*

There is a time for many words,
and there is also a time for sleep.

—*Homer*

Enjoy the present hour,
Be thankful for the past,
And neither fear nor wish
Th' approaches of the last.
—*Abraham Cowley*

This is not the end of anything,
this is the beginning of everything.
—*Ronald Reagan*

Time is the substance from which I am made. Time
is a river which carries me along, but I am the river;
it is a tiger that devours me, but I am the tiger; it is a
fire that consumes me, but I am the fire.
—*Jorge Luis Borges*

We must use time wisely and forever realize
that the time is always ripe to do right.
—*Nelson Mandela*

There is an appointed time for everything. And there is a
time for every event under heaven –
A time to give birth, and a time to die;
A time to plant, and a time to uproot what is planted.
A time to kill, and a time to heal;
A time to tear down, and a time to build up.
A time to weep, and a time to laugh;
A time to mourn, and a time to dance.
A time to throw stones, and a time to gather stones;
A time to embrace, and a time to shun embracing.
A time to search, and a time to give up as lost;
A time to keep, and a time to throw away.
A time to tear apart, and a time to sew together;
A time to be silent, and a time to speak.
A time to love, and a time to hate;
A time for war, and a time for peace.
—*adatpted from Ecclesiastes 3:1–8*

Time is the greatest innovator.
—*Francis Bacon*

What are days for?
Days are where we live.
—*Philip Larkin*

There is time for work. And time for love.
That leaves no other time.
—*Coco Chanel*

The butterfly counts not months but moments,
And has time enough.
—*Rabindranath Tagore*

Time discovered truth.
—*Lucius Annaeus Seneca*

To excel the past we must not allow ourselves
to lose contact with it; on the contrary, we must feel
it under our feet because we raised ourselves upon it.
—*José Ortega y Gasset*

Write it on your heart that everyday
is the best day of the year.
—*Ralph Waldo Emerson*

A sense of the value of time—that is, of the
best way to divide one's time into one's various
activities—is an essential preliminary to efficient work;
it is the only method of avoiding hurry.

—Arnold Bennett

Nothing great is created suddenly, any more than
a bunch of grapes or a fig. If you tell me that you
desire a fig, I answer you that there must be time.
Let it first blossom, then bear fruit, then ripen.

—Epictetus

Every day should be passed as it were our last.

—Publilius Syrus

Be intent upon the perfection of the present day.

—William Law

I have no Yesterdays.
Time took them away;
Tomorrow may not be —
But I have Today!

—Pearl Y. McGinnis

Light tomorrow with today.
—*Elizabeth Barrett Browning*

I could not know what I know today
if I weren't the age I am.
—*Anne Wilson Schael*

In my end is my beginning.
—*Mary, Queen of Scots*

Misspending a man's time is a kind of self-homicide.
—*George Savile, Marquess of Halifax*

If you trap the moment before it's ripe,
The tears of repentance you'll certainly wipe;
But if once you let the ripe moment go
You can never wipe off the tears of woe.
—*William Blake*

No time like the present.
> —*Mary de la Rivière Manley*

Tomorrow will be a new day.
> —*Miguel de Cervantes*

There is no force so powerful
as an idea whose time has come.
> —*Everett Dirksen*

There is one thing stronger than all the armies
in the world, and that is an idea whose time has come.
> —*Victor Hugo*

Time erases all things.
> —*Sophocles*

Time's glory is to calm contending kings,
To unmask falsehood and bring truth to light.
> —*William Shakespeare*

Time is an illusion, lunchtime doubly so.

—Douglas Adams

Better late than never.

—Livy

Dost thou love life? Then do not squander time;
for that's the stuff life is made of.

—Benjamin Franklin

All is well that ends well.

—John Heywood

Take joy in your yesterdays, pleasure in
your todays, and hope in your tomorrows.

—Mary Frances Ferguson

Healing is a matter of time, but it is
sometimes also a matter of opportunity.

—Hippocrates

Time is the most valuable thing a man can spend.
—*Theophrastus*

It takes a long time to bring excellence to maturity.
—*Publilius Syrus*

Time takes all and gives all.
—*Giordano Bruno*

Who knows but the world may end tonight?
—*Robert Browning*

The soul of man is immortal and imperishable.
—*Plato*

Live now, believe me, wait not till tomorrow;
Gather the roses of life today.
—*Pierre de Ronsard*

Let your life lightly dance on the edges of time like dew
on the tip of a leaf.
—*Rabindranath Tagore*

What if this present were the world's last night?
—*John Donne*

———•———

I would rather be ashes than dust! I would rather
that my spark should burn out in a brilliant blaze
than it should be stifled by dry rot. I would rather
be a superb meteor, every atom of me in magnificent
glow, than a sleepy and permanent planet. The proper
function of man is to live, not to exist. I shall not waste
my days in trying to prolong them. I shall use my time.
—*Jack London*

———•———

Think in the morning. Act in the noon.
Eat in the evening. Sleep in the night.
—*William Blake*

———•———

You will never 'find' time for anything.
If you want time you must make it.
—*Charles Buxton*

Trust

Trust yourself. You know more than you think you do.
—Benjamin Spock

———

Never be afraid to trust an
unknown future to a known god.
—Corrie ten Boom

———

A promise made is a debt unpaid.
—Robert W. Service

———

Few things help an individual more
than to place responsibility upon him
and to let him know that you trust him.
—Booker T. Washington

———

Loyalty is still the same,
Whether it win or lose the game;
True as a dial to the sun,
Although it be not shined upon.
—Samuel Butler

Trust in the Lord with all your heart,
and do not lean on your own understanding.
—adapted from Proverbs 3:5

Those who trust us, educate us.
—George Eliot

Take short views, hope for the best, and trust in God.
—Sydney Smith of Macaulay

Trust men and they will be true to you;
treat them greatly and they will show themselves great.
—Ralph Waldo Emerson

Woe to the man whose heart has not learned
while young to hope, to love—and to put its trust in life.
—Joseph Conrad

Trust only movement. Life happens at the level
of events, not of words. Trust movement.
—Alfred Adler

Trust one who has tried.

—*Virgil*

You may be deceived if you trust too much,
but you will live in torment is you don't trust enough.

—*Frank Crane*

With a person I trust I can tell her all
my problems without anyone knowing. I can
tell her all my secrets like a secret diary.

—*Priya Patel*

Just trust yourself, then you will know how to live.

—*Johann Wolfgang von Goethe*

I think that we may safely trust
a good deal more than we do.

—*Henry David Thoreau*

Never trust the teller, trust the tale.

—*D. H. Lawrence*

To be trusted is a greater compliment than to be loved.
—*George MacDonald*

Even such is Time, which takes in trust
Our youth, our joys, and all we have,
And pays us but with age and dust;
Who in the dark and silent grave,
When we have wandered all our ways,
Shuts up the story of our days:
And from which earth, and grave, and dust,
The Lord shall raise me up, I trust.
—*Sir Walter Raleigh*

Make yourself necessary to somebody.
—*Ralph Waldo Emerson*

Truth

Truth never yet fell dead in the streets; it has such affinity with the soul of man, the seed however broadcast will catch somewhere and produce its hundredfold.

—*Theodore Parker*

One truth stands firm. All that happens in world history rests on something spiritual. If the spiritual is strong, it creates world history. If it is weak, it suffers world history.

—*Albert Schweitzer*

Nothing but truth is lovely, nothing fair.

—*Nicolas Boileau-Despreaux*

Peace, if possible, but truth at any rate.

—*Martin Luther*

No pleasure is comparable to the standing upon the vantage-ground of truth.

—*Francis Bacon*

Rather than love, than money, than fame, give me truth.
—*Henry David Thoreau*

Of all feats of skill, the most
difficult is that of being honest.
—*Comtesse Diane*

Truth, crushed to earth, shall rise again.
—*William Cullen Bryant*

Be so true to thyself, as thou be not false to others.
—*Francis Bacon*

Frankness is a virtue, but too much frankness is rudeness.
—*Gotschal*

The truth is not simply what you think it is;
it is also the circumstances in which it is said,
and to whom, why, and how it is said.
—*Václav Havel*

Seeing is believing, but feeling is the truth.
—Thomas Fuller

Truth is always served by great minds, even if they fight it.
—Jean Rostand

Friends, if we be honest with ourselves,
we shall be honest with each other.
—George MacDonald

The pure and simple truth is rarely pure and never simple.
—Oscar Wilde

I believe that in the end truth will conquer.
—John Wycliffe

For my part, whatever anguish of spirit it may cost,
I am willing to know the whole truth—
to know the worst and provide for it.
—Patrick Henry

Light is the symbol of truth.
—*James Russell Lowell*

We must make the world honest before we can honestly
say to our children that honesty is the best policy.
—*George Bernard Shaw*

Never apologize for showing feeling.
When you do so, you apologize for truth.
—*Benjamin Disraeli*

Truth exists. Only lies are invented.
—*Georges Braque*

Between whom there is hearty truth, there is love.
—*Henry David Thoreau*

The spirit of truth and the spirit of
freedom—they are the pillars of society.
—*Henrik Ibsen*

The truth is more important than the facts.
—*Frank Lloyd Wright*

Pretty much all the honest truth telling
there is in the world is done by children.
—*Oliver Wendell Holmes*

The moment of truth, the sudden emergence of a new
insight, is an act of intuition. Such intuitions give the appearance of miraculous flashes, or short-circuits of reasoning. In
fact they may be likened to an immersed chain, of which
only the beginning and the end are visible above the surface
of consciousness. The diver vanishes at one end of the chain
and comes up at the other end, guided by invisible links.
—*Arthur Koestler*

Make yourself an honest man, and then you
may be sure there is one less rascal in the world.
—*Thomas Carlyle*

The greatest homage we can pay to truth, is to use it.
—*James Russell Lowell*

The naked truth is always better than the best-dressed lie.
—*Ann Landers*

Looking at his father with the sweet face
of youth brightened with the inexpressible charm
of all-conquering truth, he bravely cried out, "I can't
tell a lie. I did cut it with my hatchet."
—*George Washington*

Accuracy of statement is one of the first elements
of truth; inaccuracy is a near kin to falsehood.
—*Tryon Edwards*

The truth isn't always beauty, but the hunger for it is.
—*Nadine Gordimer*

No one means all he says and
yet very few say all they mean.
—*Henry Adams*

Truth is a child of Time.

—*Don Ford*

I had rather starve and rot and keep the privilege
of speaking the truth as I see it, than of holding all the
offices that capital has to give from the presidency down.
—*Brooks Adams*

The hero of my tale, who I love with all the power
of my soul, whom I have tried to portray in all his beauty,
who has been, is, and always will be beautiful, is Truth.
—*Leo Tolstoy*

Truth is the property of no individual
but is the treasure of all men.
—*Ralph Waldo Emerson*

Truth is what stands the test of experience.
—*Albert Einstein*

Let us begin by committing ourselves to the truth,
to see it like it is and tell it like it is, to find the truth,
to speak the truth and to live the truth.
—*Richard Nixon*

From principles is derived probability,
but truth or certainty is obtained only from facts.
—*Nathaniel Hawthorne*

For truth there is no deadline.
—*Heywood Hale Broun*

There are more truths in twenty-four hours
of a man's life than in all the philosophies.
—*Raoul Vaneigem*

The greatest friend of truth is Time, her greatest enemy
is Prejudice, and her constant companion is Humility.
—*Charles Caleb Colton*

Live truth instead of professing it.
—*Elbert Hubbard*

Chase after the truth like all hell and you'll free
yourself, even though you never touch its coattails.
—*Clarence Darrow*

It is man that makes truth great,
not truth that makes man great.

—*Confucius*

The well of true wit is truth itself.

—*George Meredith*

What is perfectly true is perfectly witty.

—*François de la Rochefoucauld*

No legacy is so rich as honesty.

—*William Shakespeare*

We shall seek the truth and endure the consequences.

—*Charles Seymour*

Each time you are honest and conduct yourself with
honesty, a success force will drive you toward greater
success. Each time you lie, even with a little white lie,
there are strong forces pushing you toward failure.

—*Joseph Sugarman*

Eternal truths will be neither true nor eternal unless
they have fresh meaning for every new social situation.
—*Franklin D. Roosevelt*

As scarce as truth is, the supply has
always been in excess of the demand.
—*Henry Wheeler Shaw*

The truth is America's most potent weapon. We
cannot enlarge upon the truth. But we can and must
intensify our efforts to make that truth more shining.
—*Richard Nixon*

Truth is the strong compost in which
beauty may sometimes germinate.
—*Christopher Morley*

Everything has to be taken on trust; truth is
only that which is taken to be true. It's the currency
of living. There may be nothing behind it, but it doesn't
make any difference so long as it is honoured.
—*Tom Stoppard*

Let us not love with words or tongue
But with actions and in truth.
—*adapted from 1 John 3:18*

Truth lies at the end of a circle.
—*Elbert Hubbard*

Truth is a jewel which should not be painted over;
but it may be set to advantage and shown in a good light.
—*George Santayana*

The well of true wit is truth itself.
—*George Meredith*

The man who fears no truths has nothing to fear from lies.
—*Thomas Jefferson*

It takes two to speak the truth—
one to speak, and another to hear.
—*Henry David Thoreau*

Man has no nobler function than to defend the truth.
—*Ruth McKenney*

Many people would be more truthful were
it not for their uncontrollable desire to talk.
—*Edgar Watson Howe*

If you tell the truth you don't have to remember anything.
—*Mark Twain*

We shall return to proven ways—not because
they are old, but because they are true.
—*Barry Goldwater*

No one can bar the road to truth, and to
advance its cause I'm ready to accept even death.
—*Aleksandr Solzhenitsyn*

I tore myself away from the safe comfort of certainties
through my love for truth; and truth rewarded me.
—*Sylvia Ashton-Warner*

Uniqueness

If a man does not keep pace with his companions, perhaps
it is because he hears a different drummer. Let him step to
the music which he hears, however measured or far away.
—*Henry David Thoreau*

Conformity is the jailer of
freedom an the enemy of growth.
—*John F. Kennedy*

All cases are unique and very similar to others.
—*T. S. Eliot*

I'm not gonna change the way I look or the
way I feel to conform to anything. I've always
been a freak. So I've been a freak all my life and I have
to live with that, you know. I'm one of those people.
—*John Lennon*

Think sideways!
—*Edward de Bono*

Sameness is the mother of disgust, variety the cure.

—Petrarch

The surest way to corrupt a youth is to instruct
him to hold in higher esteem those who think
alike than those who think differently.
—Friedrich Nietzsche

There never has been one like me before,
and there never will be one like me again.
—Howard Cosell

Originality is merely the step beyond.
—Louis Danz

Today, we have something in which is a desire for
individual recognition. We strive for recognition by trying
to achieve perfection, and we deceive ourselves into calling
the result heaven. We want whatever we do to be unique.
—Bernard Leach

Virtues

Philanthropy is almost the only virtue
which is sufficiently appreciated by mankind.
—*Henry David Thoreau*

A man oughta do what he thinks is right.
—*John Wayne*

Virtue is like a rich stone, best plain set.
—*Francis Bacon*

Virtue consists, not in abstaining
from vice, but in not desiring it.
—*George Bernard Shaw*

Gratitude is not only the greatest of virtues,
but the parent of all the others.
—*Marcus Tullius Cicero*

Virtue has its own reward, but no sale at the box office.
—*Mae West*

Let grace and goodness be the principle
loadstone of thy affections. For love which hath ends,
will have an end; whereas that which is founded
on true virtue, will always continue.
—*John Dryden*

Perfect virtue is to do unwitnessed that which
we should be capable of doing before all the world.
—*François de la Rochefoucauld*

The first virtue of a soldier is endurance
of fatigue; courage is only the second virtue.
—*Napoleon Bonaparte*

Anyone entrusted with power will abuse it if not
also animated with the love of truth and virtue.
—*Jean de la Fontaine*

A man has honour if he holds himself to
an ideal of conduct though it is inconvenient,
unprofitable or dangerous to do so.
—*Walter Lippmann*

The chief ingredients in the composition
of those qualities that gain esteem and praise,
are good nature, truth, good sense, and good breeding.
—*Joseph Addison*

Virtue is bold, and goodness never fearful.
—*William Shakespeare*

Not simply one of the virtues but
the form of every virtue at the testing point,
which means at the point of highest reality.
—*C. S. Lewis*

Humility is a virtue, and it is a virtue innate in guests.
—*Max Beerbohm*

Fame is something that must be won;
honour is something which must not be lost.
—*Arthur Schopenhauer*

I think no virtue goes with size.
—*Ralph Waldo Emerson*

Dignity does not consist in possessing
honours, but in deserving them.

—*Aristotle*

What is a weed? A plant whose virtues
have not yet been discovered.

—*Ralph Waldo Emerson*

There is no attribute of the superior man greater
than his helping men to practice virtue.

—*Mencius*

An empty bag cannot stand upright.

—*Benjamin Franklin*

Virtue extends our days: he lives
two lives who relives his past with pleasure.

—*Marcus Valerius Martialis*

The easy, gentle, and sloping path . . . is not the path
of true virtue. It demands a rough and thorny road.

—*Michel E. de Montaigne*

Mine honor is my life; both grown in one;
Take honor from me, and my life is done.
—*William Shakespeare*

A virtue to be serviceable must, like gold, be alloyed
with some commoner but more durable metal.
—*Samuel Butler*

Vice stirs up war; virtue fights.
—*Vauvenargues*

Try not to become a man of success.
Rather become a man of value.
—*Albert Einstein*

Content thyself to be obscurely good.
When vice prevails, and impious men bear sway,
The post of honour is a private station.
—*Joseph Addison*

I agree with you that there is a natural aristocracy among
men. The grounds of this are virtue and talents.
—*Thomas Jefferson*

Benevolence is the tranquil habitation of man,
and righteousness is his straight path.
—*Mencius*

Consider your origin; you were not born to live like
brutes, but to follow virtue and knowledge.
—*Dante Alighieri*

There is no road or ready way to virtue.
—*Sir Thomas Browne*

My honor is dearer to me than my life.
—*Miguel de Cervantes*

Those who labor in the earth are the
chosen people of God, if ever He had a chosen
people, whose breasts He has made His peculiar
deposit for substantial and genuine virtue.
—*Thomas Jefferson*

The gent who wakes up and finds
himself a success hasn't been asleep.
—*Wilson Mizner*

Wealth

That man is the richest whose pleasures are the cheapest.
—*Henry David Thoreau*

———

Money is like mulch, not good except to be spread.
—*Francis Bacon*

———

There is no wealth but life.
—*John Ruskin*

———

He who will not economize will have to agonize.
—*Confucius*

———

In this world it is not what we take up,
but what we give up, that makes us rich.
—*Henry Ward Beecher*

———

We owe something to extravagance, for thrift
and adventure seldom go hand in hand.
—*Jennie Jerome Churchill*

We are lovers of beauty without extravagance, and lovers of wisdom without unmanliness. Wealth to us is not mere material for vain glory but an opportunity for achievement; and poverty we think it no disgrace to acknowledge but a real degradation not to make an effort to overcome.

—Thucydides

Kissing your hand might feel very, very good but a diamond and sapphire bracelet lasts forever.

—Anita Loos

He is rich or poor according to what he is, not what he has.

—Henry Ward Beecher

The wealth of a soul is measured by how much it can feel; its poverty by how little.

—William Rounseville Alger

The only way for a rich man to be healthy is by exercise and abstinence, to live as if he were poor.

—William Temple

When prosperity comes, do not use all of it.
—*Confucius*

Make all you can, save all you can, give all you can.
—*John Wesley*

The secret point of money and power in America is neither the things that money can buy nor power for power's sake . . . but absolute personal freedom, mobility, privacy. It is the instinct which drove America to the Pacific, all through the nineteenth century, the desire to be able to find a restaurant open in case you want a sandwich, to be a free agent, live by one's own rules.
—*Joan Didion*

I'm not worried about the money,
I just want to be wonderful.
—*Marilyn Monroe*

There is a gigantic difference between earning
a great deal of money and being rich.
—*Marlene Dietrich*

You can never be too rich or too thin.
—*Duchess of Windsor*

Abstaining is favorable both to the head and to the pocket.
—*Horace Greeley*

No gentleman ever has any money.
—*Oscar Wilde*

The self-explorer, whether he wants to or not, becomes the explorer of everything else. He learns to see himself, but suddenly, provided he was honest, all the rest appears, and it is as rich as he was, and, as a final crowning, richer.
—*Elisa Canetti*

But it is pretty to see what money will do.
—*Samuel Pepys*

I don't know much about being a millionaire, but I'll bet I'd be darling at it.
—*Dorothy Parker*

I mean, the things I'm trying to do I'm still trying to do.
And having money or not having money really doesn't
help it. It doesn't interact in any way. I'm not very into
stuff. . . . After you've bought one or two things, that's it.

—*Jerry Garcia*

Get place and wealth, if possible with grace;
If not, by any means get wealth and place.

—*Alexander Pope*

Better is a little with righteousness
Than great income with injustice.

—*adapted from Proverbs 16:8*

Wealth, in even the most improbable cases,
manages to convey the aspect of intelligence.

—*John Kenneth Galbraith*

There must be a reason why some people can
afford to live well. They must have worked for it.
I only feel angry when I see waste. When I see
people throwing away things that we could use.

—*Mother Teresa*

457

A good reputation is more valuable than money.
—*Publilius Syrus*

I glory more in the coming purchase
of my wealth than in the glad possession.
—*Ben Jonson*

The first wealth is health.
—*Ralph Waldo Emerson*

Money is not everything, but it is
better than having one's health.
—*Woody Allen*

Money is only money, beans tonight and steak tomorrow.
So long as you can look yourself in the eye.
—*Meridel LeSueur*

Money doesn't make you happy. I now have $50
but I was just as happy when I had $48 million.
—*Arnold Schwarzenegger*

It is better to live rich than to die rich.
—*Samuel Johnson*

Sleep, riches and health to be truly
enjoyed must be interrupted.
—*Jean Paul Richter*

The only question of wealth is what you do with it.
—*John D. Rockefeller III*

Money buys food, clothes, houses, land, guns,
jewels, men, women, time to be lazy and listen to music.
Money buys everything except love, personality,
freedom, immortality, silence, peace.
—*Carl Sandburg*

Riches do not consist in the possession
of treasures, but in the use made of them.
—*Napoleon Bonaparte*

The smell of profit is clean and sweet, whatever the source.
—*Juvenal*

It is not the man who has too little,
but the man who craves more, that is poor.

—*Lucius Annaeus Seneca*

A little house well filled, a little field well tilled,
and a little wife well willed, are great riches.

—*Benjamin Franklin*

I've been rich and I've been poor.
Believe me, rich is better.

—*Sophie Tucker*

He that maketh haste to be rich shall not be innocent.

—*adapted from Proverbs 28:20*

Wisdom & Knowledge

There is wisdom of the head,
and . . . a wisdom of the heart.

—*Charles Dickens*

It is knowledge that influences and equalizes
the social condition of man; that gives to all, however
different their political position, passions which are
in common, and enjoyments which are universal.

—*Benjamin Disraeli*

And wit's the noblest frailty of the mind.

—*Thomas Shadwell*

Blest the man who possesses a keen intelligent mind.

—*Aristophanes*

Knowledge is power.

—*Francis Bacon*

Wisdom begins in wonder.

—Socrates

We owe almost all our knowledge not to those
who have agreed, but to those who have suffered.

—Charles Caleb Colton

The wise man doesn't give the right answers,
he poses the right questions.

—Claude Levi-Strauss

Wise man: One who sees the storm
coming before the clouds appear.

—Elbert Hubbard

As knowledge increases, wonder deepens.

—Charles Morgan

An intellectual is a person who has discovered
something more interesting than sex.

—Aldous Huxley

Wisdom is not to be obtained from textbooks, but must
be coined out of human experience in the flame of life.
—*Morris Raphael Cohen*

The more extensive a man's knowledge of what has been
done, the greater will be his power of knowing what to do.
—*Benjamin Disraeli*

If a man empties his purse into his head,
no one can take it from him. An investment
in knowledge always pays the best interest.
—*Benjamin Franklin*

I have taken all knowledge to be my province.
—*Francis Bacon*

There is no knowledge that is not power.
—*Ralph Waldo Emerson*

Knowledge cultivates your seeds
and does not sow in your seeds.
—*Kahlil Gibran*

Eloquence is the child of knowledge.
—*Benjamin Disraeli*

One of the greatest joys known to man is to take
a flight into ignorance in search of knowledge.
—*Robert Lynd*

The fox knows many things—the hedgehog one big thing.
—*Archilochus*

The wisest man is generally he
who thinks himself the least so.
—*Nicolas Boileau-Despreaux*

You can tell whether a man is clever by his answers.
You can tell whether a man is wise by his questions.
—*Naquib*

The is much pleasure to be
gained from useless knowledge.
—*Bertrand Russell*

To know when to be generous
and when firm—this is wisdom.
—*Elbert Hubbard*

It is a characteristic of wisdom not to do desperate things.
—*Henry David Thoreau*

The road to wisdom? Well it's plain
And simple to express:
Err
And Err
And err again
But less
And less
And less.

—*Piet Hein*

The art of being wise is the art
of knowing what to overlook.
—*William James*

A wise man gets more use from his
enemies than a fool from his friends.
—*Baltasar Gracian*

465

Not to know certain things is a great part of wisdom.
—*Hugo Grotius*

It is characteristic of wisdom not to do desperate things.
—*Henry David Thoreau*

I do not believe that sheer suffering teaches.
If suffering along taught, all the world would be wise,
since everyone suffers. To suffering must be added
mourning, understanding, patience, love, openness
and the willingness to remain vulnerable.
—*Anne Morrow Lindbergh*

He dares to be a fool, and that is the
first step in the direction of wisdom.
—*James G. Huneker*

Nine-tenths of wisdom consists in being wise in time.
—*Theodore Roosevelt*

It is not wise to be wiser than necessary.
—*Philippe Quinault*

All human wisdom is summed
up in two words—wait and hope.
——*Alexandre Dumas the Elder*

Knowledge comes, but wisdom lingers.
——*Lord Tennyson*

It requires wisdom to understand wisdom;
the music is nothing if the audience is deaf.
——*Walter Lippmann*

Every man is a damn fool for at least five minutes
every day. Wisdom consists in not exceeding the limit.
——*Elbert Hubbard*

In all affairs, love, religion, politics or business,
it's a healthy idea, now and then, to hang a question
mark on things you have long taken for granted.
——*Bertrand Russell*

Knowledge can be communicated but not wisdom.
——*Hermann Hesse*

Knowledge of what is possible
is the beginning of happiness.
—*George Santayana*

Intelligence is derived from two words—inter and legere—
inter meaning "between" and legere meaning "to choose."
An intelligent person, therefore, is one who has learned
"to choose between." He knows that good is better than
evil, that confidence should supercede fear, that love
is superior to hate, that gentleness is better than cruelty,
forbearance than intolerance, compassion than arrogance,
and that truth has more virtue than ignorance.
—*J. Martin Klotsche*

The simplest questions are the hardest to answer.
—*Northrop Frye*

Knowledge alone is not enough. It must be leavened
with magnanimity before it becomes wisdom.
—*Adlai E. Stevenson*

Zeal without knowledge is fire without light.
—*Thomas Fuller*

All zeal runs down. What replaces it? Intellectualism.
—*Arthur R. M. Lower*

All men by nature desire knowledge.
—*Aristotle*

Not ignorance, but ignorance
of ignorance is the death of knowledge.
—*Alfred North Whitehead*

Real knowledge is to know the extent of one's ignorance.
—*Confucius*

Clever men are impressed in their differences
from their fellows. Wise men are conscious
of their resemblance to them.
—*R. H. Tawney*

The highest intellects, like the tops of mountains,
are the first to catch and to reflect the dawn.
—*Thomas Babington Macaulay*

My mind to me a kingdom is;
Such present joys therein I find
That is excels all other bliss
That earth affords or grows by kind:
Though much I want which most would have,
Yet still my mind forbids to crave.

—Sir Edward Dyer

No man is wise enough by himself.

—Titus Maccius Plautus

There is a wisdom in this beyond the rules of physic.
A man's own observation, what he finds good of and
what he finds hurt of, is the best physic to preserve health.

—Francis Bacon

The wise learn many things from their enemies.

—Aristophanes

Some men have only one book
in them; others, a library.

—Sydney Smith of Macaulay

Cherish that which is within you, and shut off that
which is without, for much knowledge is a curse.
—*Chuang-tzu*

Think for yourself and let others enjoy
the privilege of doing so too.
—*Voltaire*

Good to be merry and wise.
—*John Heywood*

Nothing is more terrible than ignorance in action.
—*Johann Wolfgang von Goethe*

The improvement of understanding is for two ends:
first, our own increase of knowledge; secondly,
to enable us to deliver that knowledge to others.
—*John Locke*

I do not think much of a man who
is not wiser today than he was yesterday.
—*Abraham Lincoln*

It is worse still to be ignorant of your ignorance.
—St. Jerome

Let every slice of knowledge
be opened and set a-flowing.
—John Adams

Knowledge is proud that he has learn'd so much;
Wisdom is humble that he knows no more.
—William Cowper

Our greatest battles are that with our own minds.
—Jameson Frank

Be wisely worldly, be not worldly wise.
—Francis Quarles

A good mind possesses a kingdom.
—Lucius Annaeus Seneca

Early to bed and early to rise,
makes a man healthy, wealthy and wise.
—*Benjamin Franklin*

Be wise; Soar not too high to fall; but stoop to rise.
—*Philip Massinger*

To know
That which before us lies in daily life
Is the prime wisdom.
—*John Milton*

It is not enough to have a good mind.
The main thing is to use it well.
—*René Descartes*

Wisdom outweighs any wealth.
—*Sophocles*

Beware when the great God
lets loose a thinker on this planet.
—*Ralph Waldo Emerson*

There is only one good,
knowledge, and one evil, ignorance.

—Socrates

Will and Intellect are one and the same thing.
—Benedict Spinoza

Wit and wisdom are born with a man.
—John Seldon

Let my heart be wise. It is the gods' best gift.
—Euripides

The World

The world and my being, its life and mine, were one.
The microcosm and macrocosm were at length atoned,
at length in harmony. I lived in everything;
everything entered and lived here.
—*George MacDonald*

The world is a looking glass and gives back
to every man the reflection of his own face.
—*William Makepeace Thackeray*

It is only in marriage with the world that our ideals
can bear fruit; divorced form it, they remain barren.
—*Bertrand Russell*

The world belongs to the energetic.
—*Henry David Thoreau*

The world is all gates, all opportunities,
strings of tension waiting to be struck.
—*Ralph Waldo Emerson*

The world is not yet exhausted; let me see
something tomorrow which I never saw before.
—*Samuel Johnson*

There is nothing on earth divine except humanity.
—*Walter Savage Landor*

The earth is given as a common
for men to labor and live in.
—*Thomas Jefferson*

Our earth is but a small star in a great universe.
Yet of it we can make, if we choose, a planet unvexed
by war, untroubled by hunger or fear, undivided by
senseless distinctions of race, color or theory.
—*Stephen Vincent Benét*

In the old world that is passing, in the new world
that is coming, national efficiency has been and will
be a controlling factor in national safety and welfare.
—*Gifford Pinchot*

Our country is the world—our countrymen are mankind.
——*William Lloyd Garrison*

I hate nobody; I am in charity with the whole world.
——*Jonathan Swift*

Don't ask yourself what the world needs; ask yourself what makes you come alive. And then go and do that. Because what the world needs is people who have come alive.
——*Harold Whitman*

Earth, thou great footstool of our God, who reigns on high; though fruitful source of all our raiment, life, and food; our house, our parent, and our nurse.
——*Isaac Watts*

I have no country to fight for: my country is the earth, and I am a citizen of the world.
——*Eugene V. Debs*

The world is my country, all mankind
are my brethren, and to do good is my religion.
—*Thomas Paine*

It's a funny old world.
—*Margaret Thatcher*

The world you desired can be won.
It exists, it is real, it is possible, it is yours.
—*Ayn Rand*

The world is not black and white.
More like black and grey.
—*Graham Greene*

Bibliography

Adler, Bill, and Fred Astaire. *A Wonderful Life*. New York: Carroll & Graf Publishers, Inc., 1987.

Andrews, Robert. *Cassell Dictionary of Contemporary Quotations*. London: Cassell, 1996.

Augarde, Tom, ed. *The Oxford Dictionary of Modern Quotations*. Oxford: Oxford University Press, 1991.

Ball, Lucille. *Love, Lucy*. New York: G. P. Putnam's Sons, 1996.

Bartlett, John, and Justin Kaplan, eds. *Bartlett's Familiar Quotations*. Boston: Little, Brown and Company, 1992.

Beilenson, Helen, and Peter Beilenson, eds. *The Widsom and Wit of Franklin D. Roosevelt*. New York: Peter Pauper Press, Inc., 1982.

Bibliography

Bolander, Donald O. *The New Webster's Quotation Dictionary*. Toronto: Lexicon Publications, 1987.

Burns, George. *Gracie*. New York: Penguin Books, 1988.

Byrne, Robert. *The Fourth and By Far the Most Recent 637 Best Things A New Yorkbody Ever Said*. New York: Atheneum, 1990.

Cannon, Elaine. *Notable Quotables from Women to Women*. Salt Lake City: Bookcraft, 1992.

Cher. *The First Time.* New York: Simon & Schuster, 1998.

Davis, Kathy. *The Time to Be Happy Is Now*, San Rafael, CA: Cedco Publishing Compay, 1999.

Doherty, Paul C. *King Arthur*. New York: Chelsea House Publishers, 1987.

Donadio, Stephen, et al. *The New York Public Library Book of Twentieth-Century American Quotations.* New York: Warner Books, Inc., 1992.

Editors of *Rolling Stone. Garcia.* Boston: Little, Brown and Company, 1995.

Exley, Helen. *The Love Between Friends.* Hertfordshire, England: Exley Publications, 2000.

Fay, Jim, and Charles Fay. *Love and Logic Magic for Early Childhood.* Golden, CO: The Love and Logic Press, Inc., 2000.

Fitzhenry, Robert I. ed. *The Harper Book of Quotations.* New York: Harper Perennial, 1993.

Furbee, Mary, and Mike Furbee. *The Importance of Mohandas Gandhi.* San Diego: Lucent Books, 2000.

inspirationpeak.com

Lesman, Helen. *Heart to Heart*. Minneapolis: Northwestern Productions, Inc., 1988.

Merylstreeponline.net

Oprah.com

Partington, Angela, ed. *The Oxford Dictionary of Quotations*. Oxford: Oxford University Press, 1992.

Prayers and Promises for Women, a Topical Devotional. Nashville, TN: Lifeway Christian Stores, 2003.

Prochnow, Herbert V. *Speaker's & Toastmaster's Handbook*. Rocklin, CA: Prima Publishing & Communnications, 1990.

QuotationsPage.com

Quoteland.com

Rees, Nigel. *Cassell Companion to Quotations*. New York: Cassell, 1997.

Reiter, Mary Jo. *Weaving a Life: The Story of Mary Meigs Atwater*. Loveland, CO: Interweave Press, 1992.

Resnick, Jane Parker. *Love and Friendship*. Stamford, CT: Longmeadow Press, 1992.

Ryrie, Charles C. *New American Standard The Ryrie Study Bible*. Chicago: Moody Publishers, 2003.

Safire, William. *Lend Me Your Ears: Great Speeches in History*. New York: W.W. Norton & Company, 1992.

Senn, J. A. *Quotations for Kids*. Brookfield, CT: The Millbrook Press, 1999.

Sunshine, Linda, ed. *Words of Comfort*. New York: Smallwood and Stewart, Inc., 1996.

Weislang, Barbara. *Susan B. Anthony*. New York: Chelsea House Publishers, 1988.

Wepman, Dennis. *Alexander the Great*. New York: Chelsea House Publishers, 1986.

Wukovits, John F. *George W. Bush*. San Diego, CA: Lucent Books, 2000.

Index

Abdul-Jabbar, Kareem . . . 144

Acheson, Dean 170

Acton, Lord 132

Adams, Abigail 109, 121

Adams, Brooks 439

Adams, Douglas 426

Adams, George Matthew
. . . . 78

Adams, Henry 121, 438

Adams, John 331, 472

Adams, Samuel 314, 361

Adathon 199

Addams, Jane 61, 204

Addison, Joseph 99, 199,
200, 237, 323, 327, 449, 451

Ade, George 282

Adler, Alfred 430

Adorno, Theodor W. . . .183

Aesop 254, 397

Agee, James 90

Aiken, George 110

Akenside, Mark 46

Alcott, Amos Bronson 72

Alden, Robert 314

Aldrich, Thomas Bailey . . . 26,
299

Aldrin, Buzz 299

Alexander the Great 56

Alexander, Cecil Frances
. . . . 200

Alexander, Lloyd 403

Alger, William Rounseville
. . . . 454

Ali, Muhammad 164, 231,
371, 418

Alighieri, Dante 229, 377,
452

Allen, Elizabeth Akers 87

Allen, James 172

Allen, Woody 303, 383,
397, 458

Allport, Gordon 25

Amiel, Henri Frédéric . . . 15,
24, 58, 77, 176

Anderson, Lindsay 34

Andrew, Prince 243

Andrus, Ethel Percy 177,
210

Angeli, Marguerite de . . . 397

Angelou, Maya . . . 57, 97, 184,
256, 345

Anonymous 134

Anouilh, Jean 45, 48

Anthony, Susan B. . . .135, 262

Index

Antiphanes 82

Antoninus, Marcus Aurelius
57, 170, 202, 218, 306, 350, 381

Antrim, Minna 139, 140, 175

Arbus, Diane 244

Archard, Marcel 374

Archilochus 464

Archimedes 186

Arendt, Hannah 136

Aristophanes 27, 82, 387, 392, 470

Aristotle . . . 12, 47, 72, 82, 89, 109, 117, 158, 164, 214, 273, 276, 292, 306, 348, 354, 362, 450, 469

Armstrong, John 55

Armstrong, Neil 145, 279

Armstrong, William H. . . 338

Arnauld, Angelique 193

Arno, Peter 343

Arnold, Matthew 11, 77, 134, 190, 213, 300, 353, 386

Arp, Jean 33

Ash, Mary Kay 313, 314

Ashe, Arthur 181

Ashton-Warner, Sylvia . . . 444

Asimov, Isaac 65

Asquith, Herbert 203

Astor, Lady Nancy . . . 64, 117, 120

Athens, Menander of 127

Atkinson, John 268

Atwater, Mary Meigs 296

Auden, W. H. 23, 176, 255

Augustine, St . . . 85, 184, 197, 199, 240, 250, 289

Austen, Jane 313, 384

Avot, Pirke 369

Bachelard, Gaston 226

Bacon, Francis 118, 183, 242, 247, 251, 296, 302, 306, 421, 433, 434, 447, 453, 461, 463, 470

Baden-Powell,
Sir Robert 349

Baeck, Leo 25

Bagehot, Walter 282

Bailey, P. J. 41

Bailey, Pearl 58

Bailey, Philip 251

Baker, James 417

Bakker, Jim 141

Baldwin, Christina 61

Ball, Lucille 12, 15, 90, 102, 128, 288, 318

Balzac, Honoré de 345

Bankhead, Tallulah 76

Barnes, Djuna 106

Barrie, James Matthew . . . 88, 166, 180, 268, 353

Barth, Joseph 353

Barth, Karl 260

Barton, Bruce 71

Baruch, Bernard 20, 76, 365

Barzun, Jacques 121

Baudelaire, Charles 130, 205

Baudrillard, Jean 259

Beal, Frances M. 62

Beard, Charles A. 314

Bearden, Romare 38

Beaumarchais 75

Becker, Mary Lamberton 26

Beckett, Samuel 304

Beecher, Henry Ward 42, 77, 180, 193, 220, 231, 287, 317, 340, 453, 454

Beerbohm, Max 449

Behan, Brendan 100

Behn, Aphra 167, 313

Beisser, Arnold 16

Bell, Bernard Iddings 120

Bell, Elliot V. 135

Belushi, John 20

Benchley, Robert 373

Benét, Stephen Vincent . . .476

Bengis, Ingrid 236

Bennett, Alan 268

Bennett, Arnold 423

Bergson, Henri 399

Berle, Milton 407

Berlin, Irving 391

Bernard, Dorothy 51, 278

Bible
1 Corinthians 13:13 . . . 294
1 Corinthians 16:13 12
1 John 3:18 443
Acts 20:35 182
Ecclesiastes 3:1–8 421
Ecclesiastes 7:8 325
Ephesians 4:2 233
Ephesians 4:32 232
Genesis 15:15 17
John 8:12 187
John 15:12 284
Leviticus 19:18 284
Matthew 5:42 181
Matthew 7:12 252
Proverbs 3:5 430
Proverbs 9:9 107
Proverbs 16:8 457
Proverbs 16:9 194
Proverbs 28:1 52
Proverbs 28:20 460
Psalms 139:9–10 196

Index

Romans 6:23 364
Titus 2:2–3 19
Bierce, Ambrose 119
Billings, Josh 140, 175,
  242, 260, 320, 341, 375
Bird, Larry 192
Bird, Rose 248
Bisset, Jacqueline 44
Blackstone, William 247
Blake, William . . . 14, 167, 173,
  200, 293, 305, 307, 385, 424,
  428
Blessington, Lady 45
Blishen, Edward 114
Bliss, Daniel 152
Bloom, Allan 114, 122
Blos, Joan W. 274
Boardman,
  George Dana 72, 295
Boethius 291
Bohr, Niels 373
Boileau-Despreaux,
  Nicolas 433, 464
Bok, Derek 118
Bonaparte, Napoleon 36,
  235, 334, 448, 459
Bonaventure, St. 397
Bono, Edward de 445
Boom, Corrie ten . . 202,429
Boorstin, Daniel J. 219

Booth,
  Maud Ballington 180
Borenstein, Jeffrey 148
Borge, Victor 259
Borges, Jorge Luis 420
Borland, Hal 64
Boswell, James 163
Boswell, Nelson 387
Bovee,
  Christian Nestell . 30, 254
Bradley, Omar 51
Braiker, Harriet 187
Branagh, Kenneth 159
Brandeis, Louis D. 111,
  154, 261, 282
Branden, Nathaniel 370
Branden, Samuel 221
Braque, Georges 436
Breathnach, Sarah Ban . . . 211
Brecht, Bertolt 273
Brilliant, Ashleigh 277
Bristol, Claude M. 129
Brontë, Charlotte 87
Brontë, Emily 49
Brookner, Anita 285
Brothers, Joyce 283, 361
Brougham,
  Henry Peter 119
Broun,
  Heywood Hale . . .79, 440

Brown, Bob 395
Brown, H. Jackson, Jr. 241
Brown, James 394
Brown, Pam 161, 383
Browne, Sir Thomas 235, 452
Browning, Elizabeth
    Barrett . . 172, 193, 233, 424
Browning, Robert 19, 69, 85, 295, 313, 330, 345, 347, 381, 395, 427
Bruno, Giordano 427
Bryan,
    William Jennings 146
Bryant,
    William Cullen 434
Buchan, John 213, 232
Buck, Pearl S. 91, 290
Buddha 215
Buffon, Comte de . . .323, 324
Bulwer-Lytton, Edward . . .78, 105, 336
Burke, Edmund 238, 250, 332
Burnett, Leo 189
Burns, George 167, 272
Burns, Robert 302
Burroughs, John 25, 178, 299, 301
Burt, Benjamin 368

Burton, Robert 233, 234 379
Buscaglia, Leo 201
Bush, Barbara 359
Bush, George H. W. . .59, 405
Bush, George W. 110
Butler, Samuel 28, 290, 429, 451
Buxton, Charles 382, 388, 428
Byrnes, James Francis 157
Byron, Lord 89, 216, 277, 383
Caesar, Julius 404
Cahn, Peggy 15, 17
Caine, Michael 140
Campbell, Joseph 21, 210
Campbell,
    Mrs. Patrick 363
Camus, Albert 139, 210, 216
Canetti, Elisa 456
Cardozo, Benjamin 151, 247
Carlet, Pierre 254
Carlyle, Thomas 54, 102, 175, 193, 255, 279, 281, 303, 325, 359, 376, 380, 408, 437
Carman, Bliss 346, 387
Carnegie, Andrew 343

Index

Carnegie, Dale 339
Carr, J.L. 108
Carrel, Alexis 11
Carroll, Lewis . . . 13, 104, 237, 283, 352
Carson, Rachel 93
Carter, Hodding, Jr. 97
Carter, Jimmy 64, 152
Carver,
    George Washington . . .298
Cary, Joyce 278
Cassady, Neal 41
Casson, Herbert N. 389
Cather, Willa 213, 302
Catherine of Siena, St. . .348
Catt, Carrie Chapman . . . 248
Cavafy, C. P. 244
Cavell, Edith 329
Celan, Paul 296
Cervantes, Miguel de 50, 51, 81, 135, 254, 312, 378, 425, 452
Chalmers, Allan K. 212
Chamfort,
    Sebastien Roch 255
Chanel, Coco . . . 27, 213, 422
Channing, William Ellery
    . . . . 143, 287
Chapman, George . . . 28, 151
Chase, Alexander 395

Cher 19, 316
Chester, Henry 80
Chesterfield, Lord 75, 185
Chesterton, G. K. 217, 363, 385
Chevalier, Maurice 17
Chicago, Judy 112
Christina,
    Queen of Sweden 364
Chuang-tzu 471
Churchill,
    Jennie Jerome 453
Churchill, Winston . . . 51, 52, 129, 171, 172, 205, 347, 370, 384
Cicero, Marcus Tullius . . . 128, 161, 163, 188, 189, 376, 378, 381, 447
Cioran, E. M. 103
Clark, Frank A. 256
Clark, Ramsey 66, 92
Clarke, Arthur C. 280
Clay, Henry 371
Clemenceau, Georges . . . 376
Cleaver, Bill 404
Cleaver, Vera 404
Cohen,
    Morris Raphael 463
Coleridge,
    David Hartley 152

Colton, Charles Caleb 59, 61, 440, 462

Comte, Auguste 191

Comtesse Diane 434

Conant, James Bryant ... 261, 411

Confucius 123, 126, 441, 453, 455, 469

Connolly, Cyril 214, 352

Conrad, Joseph 125

Cooley, Charles Horton ... 32

Cooley, Mason 411

Coolidge, Calvin ... 328, 340, 356, 380

Cordes, Liane 123

Corneille, Pierre 52, 182, 371, 409, 415

Cosby, Bill 388

Cosell, Howard 52

Cousins, Norman 112

Covey, Stephen 236

Coward, Noel 245

Cowley, Abraham 420

Cowper, William ... 186, 197, 212, 244, 272, 472

Cox, Coleman 343

Crashaw, William 175

Crassus, Marcus Licinius 187

Crisp, Quentin 362

Crockett, David 399

Cronyn, Hume 18

Crowfoot 269

Cumberland, Richard ... 406

cummings, e. e. 79, 260, 297, 367

Curtis, George William ... 17, 327

Dangerfield, Rodney 13

Daniels, R. G. 311

Danz, Louis 446

Darnell, Linda 390

Darrow, Clarence ... 249, 440

Davies, Robertson 169, 260

Davis, Bette 123

Davis, Elmer 52

Day, Lillian 72

Dayan, Moshe 147

Debs, Eugene V. 63, 477

Dekker, Thomas 130

de Clapiers, Luc 127, 191, 208

de Gautier, Jules 236

de Gaulle, Charles 207, 375

de Mille, Agnes 38, 146

de Musset, Alfred 203

de Sales, St. Francis 325

de Vries, Peter 139

Index

Demosthenes 99

Depardieu, Gérard 243

Descartes, René 473

Dewey, John 58

Dewey, Orville 125

Dickens, Charles 78, 115,
   257, 350, 412, 417, 461

Dickinson, Emily 44, 115,
   223, 240, 276, 279

Dickinson, Mary Lowe . . . 361

Didion, Joan 455

Dietrich, Marlene 455

Diller, Phyllis 315

Dirksen, Everett 425

Disney, Walt 97, 230

Disraeli, Benjamin 23, 69,
   73, 101, 104, 221, 267, 388,
   395, 403, 436, 461, 463, 464

Dobson, Shirley 194

Doherty, Henry 62

Donne, John 369, 428

Douglas,
   Helen Gahagan 74

Douglas, William O. 113

Doyle, Arthur Conan 116

Dreiser, Theodore 38, 116

Drucker, Peter F. 112

Dryden, John 53, 54, 168,
   346, 366, 448

Du Bois, W. E. B. 46, 111,
   113, 263, 266

Dubuffet, Jean 40

Duchess of Windsor 456

Dumas, Alexandre
   the Elder 357, 467

Duncan, Sara Jeannette . . . 259

Dewey, John 58

Dyer, Sir Edward 470

Dylan, Bob 220, 229

Earhart, Amelia 70

Eastman, Crystal 134

Eastman, Max 32

Eckert, Allan W. 84

Edelman,
   Marion Wright 178

Edison, Thomas 126, 190

Edwards, Oliver 312

Edwards, Tryon 18, 188,
   438

Ehrenreich, Barbara 130

Ehrlich, Gretel 299

Ehrmann, Max 24, 305,
   310, 377

Einstein, Albert 77, 93,
   113, 114, 117, 174, 180, 182,
   235, 439, 451

Eisenhower, Dwight D. . . . 79,
   92, 149, 249, 336, 350

Eliot, Charles W. 169

Eliot, George 160, 190, 251, 355, 361, 379, 430

Eliot, T. S. 232, 416

Elliot, Henry Rutherford . . .257

Ellis, Havelock 139, 358

Ellis, James 44

Ellison, Ralph 42, 360

el-Sadat, Anwar 101

Emerson, Ralph Waldo . . . 26, 43, 45, 61, 67, 71, 76, 80, 95, 110, 113, 139, 145, 155, 158, 160, 163, 165, 173, 174, 179, 181, 182, 184, 186, 188, 189, 193, 195, 196, 198, 201, 205, 206, 211, 219, 220, 222, 230, 252, 269, 273, 292, 302, 315, 324, 333, 335, 346, 354, 355, 356, 359, 361, 363, 364, 365, 385, 398, 400, 402, 413, 415, 422, 430, 432, 439, 449, 450, 458, 463, 473, 475

Ephron, Nora 43

Epictetus 115, 148, 200, 214, 380, 406, 423

Epicurus 166, 215

Erasmus, Desiderius 282

Erikson, Erik H. 134

Essex, Lord 175

Euripides 198, 375, 474

Evans, Richard L. 212

Everett, Edward 107

Evers, Medgar 67

Ewing, Sam 129

Fadiman, Clifton 384

Farrell, Joseph 138

Faulkner, William 185

Fawcett, Millicent Garrett 54

Fay, Charles 315, 317, 318, 321, 391

Fay, Jim 315, 317, 318, 321, 391

Fénelon, François de Salignac de la Mothe- 375

Ferguson, Mary Frances 426

Finley, John 25

Firestone, Harry 357

Fisher, Dorothy Canfield 319

Fitzgerald, F. Scott 26

Fitzgerald, Zelda 283

Fitzhugh, Louise 404

Flavia 227

Fleming, Ian 414

Florio, John 303

Index

Foley, Elisabeth 162

Fontaine, Jean de la 323, 325, 448

Forbes, Bertie Charles . . . 125

Forbes, Malcolm 75

Ford, Betty 279

Ford, Don 438

Ford, Henry 24, 88, 93

Ford, Henry, II 171

Forster, E. M. 34

Fox, Emmet 267

France, Anatole 235, 403

Frank, Anne 86

Frank, Jameson 472

Frankl, Viktor 418

Franklin, Benjamin 83, 111, 140, 166, 173, 197, 214, 247, 325, 337, 339, 405, 426, 450, 460, 463, 473

French, Marilyn 35

Freud, Clement 384

Friedman, Milton . . . 136, 147

Friedman, Rose 136

Fromm, Erich 143, 183, 290, 351

Frost, Robert 115, 129, 209, 285, 286, 412

Froude, James A. 80

Frye, Northrop 468

Fuller, Thomas 103, 118, 162, 204, 308, 435, 468

Galbraith, John Kenneth 457

Galileo 108

Galsworthy, John 75

Gandhi 60, 143, 149, 160, 196, 281, 288, 365, 400, 407, 417

Gandhi, Indira 377

Garbett, Archbishop C. . .103

Garcia, Jerry 105, 347, 391, 410, 413, 457

Garfield, James A. . . . 15, 120, 128

Garrison, William Lloyd 477

Gaskell, Elizabeth Cleghorn . . .351

Gawain, Shakti 142

George, David Lloyd 50

Giacomini, Lynwood L. 300

Gibbon, Edward 138

Gibbons, James Cardinal. 64

Giblin, Frank J. 370

Gibran, Kahlil . . . 45, 62, 142, 156, 177, 179, 185, 400, 463

Gide, André 32, 37, 409

Gildersleeve, Virginia 115

Ginsberg, Louis 289

Giovanni, Nikki 362

Glasgow, Ellen 19

Godard, Jean-Luc 33

Goddard, Robert H. . . .228

Goethe, Johann Wolfgang von 70, 84, 85, 95, 174, 189, 209, 226, 230, 264, 271, 308, 317, 335, 359, 369, 380, 386, 401, 404, 407, 417, 431, 471

Goldman, Emma 87

Goldsmith, Oliver 403

Goldwater, Barry . . . 132, 249, 444

Goldwyn, Samuel . . . 127, 289

Goodman, Joel 256

Goodman, Paul 245, 382

Gordimer, Nadine 438

Gordon, Ruth 342

Gorky, Maxim 288

Gossage, Howard 310

Gotschal 434

Gracian, Baltasar 465

Graham, Billy 258, 293

Graham, Katherine 130

Grandma Moses 274

Grant, Ulysses S. 336

Granville, George 182

Grass, Günter 37

Gray, Charlotte 160

Greeley, Horace 456

Green, Matthew 168

Greene, Graham 478

Greer, Germaine 21

Gregg, Alan 110

Gregory, Dick 95

Gretzky, Wayne 415

Grotius, Hugo 466

Guizot, François 13

Gurdjieff, George 107

Hagen, Jean 167

Hale, Edward Everett 329

Hale, Nathan 327

Halifax, Lord 414

Hall, William 359

Halm, Friedrich 290

Hammarskjöld, Dag 246

Hand, Learned 250, 266

Hannibal 417

Hardy, Thomas 140, 311, 324, 378

Harlan, John Marshall . . . 133

Harriman, Edward H. . . .171

Harrington, Michael 330

Harrison, Barbara Grizzuti 236

Index

Havel, Václav 225

Hawes, Joel 186

Hawking, Stephen 342

Hawthorne, Nathaniel . . . 440

Hay, John 300

Hayes, Helen 39, 285

Hazlitt, William 141, 173, 261, 341, 380

Heatter, Gabriel 419

Hedge, H. F. 226

Heilbrun, Carolyn 419

Hein, Piet 465

Helprin, Mark 297

Helvetius, Claude Adrien 167

Hemingway, Ernest 371, 387

Henderson, Nelson 270

Henry, Matthew 314

Henry, Patrick 137, 172, 264, 435

Heraclitus 69

Herbert, A. P. 197

Herbert, George . . . 161, 162, 311, 318

Herodotus 166, 414

Herold, Don 79, 88, 108, 125

Herrick, Robert 352

Hesburgh, Theodore 317

Hesiod 130

Hesse, Hermann 467

Heywood, John 128, 203, 414, 426, 471

Highet, Gilbert 206

Highwater, Jamake 39

Hill, Napoleon 223, 339

Hippocrates . . . 183, 202, 426

Hitchcock, Raymond . . . 256

Hoagland, Edward 258

Hocking, William Ernest 18

Hoffman, Abbie 236

Hoffman, Paul 334, 390

Holiday, Billie 391

Holland, J. G. 62

Holmes, John Andrew . . . 363

Holmes, Oliver Wendell 22, 86, 189, 244, 270, 273, 279, 437

Holt, John 73

Homer 16, 195, 202, 204, 231, 322, 353, 420

Hooper, Ellen Sturgis 408

Hoover, Herbert 89, 402

Horace 127, 310, 419

Howe, Edgar Watson 155, 255, 390, 444

Hubbard, Elbert . . . 22, 28, 39, 99, 108, 129, 137, 151, 174,

206, 240, 271, 287, 308, 310,
394, 440, 443, 462, 465, 467
Hubbard, Kin 47
Hudson, Burke 239
Hudson,
   William Henry 206
Hugo, Victor 121, 256,
294, 304, 425
Hulbert, Harold 317
Hull, Cordell 148
Hume, David 48
Humphrey, Hubert H. . . . 133,
328
Huneker, James G. . . . 36, 227,
466
Hunter, Lucretia P. 389
Huxley, Aldous 70, 138,
191, 379, 462
Huxley, Thomas 113
Ibsen, Henrik 53, 94, 170,
299, 365, 436
Ingalls, Brian 302
Ingersoll,
   Robert Green 49, 108,
215, 262
Ionesco, Eugène 36, 206
Irenaeus, St. 198
Irving, Washington 188,
253, 308, 339
Jackson, Andrew 53

Jackson, Jesse 67, 322
Jackson, Phil 215
Jaffe, Sam 253
James, Edmund Storer 23
James, Henry 267
James, P. D. 127
James, William 109, 142,
274, 465
Jameson, Storm 210
Jefferson, Thomas 28,
50, 131, 262, 263, 443, 451,
452, 476
Jenks, Earlene Larson 54
Jerome, St. 472
Jimenez, Juan Ramon 66
John XXIII, Pope 64
John Paul II, Pope 91
Johnson, Claudia
   (Lady Bird) 40
Johnson, Earvin (Magic) . . . 96
Johnson, Lyndon B. 55,
334, 337, 353, 360, 370
Johnson, Samuel 99,
102, 126, 156, 185, 220, 235,
243, 309, 340, 353, 360, 390,
459, 476
Johnson, William H. 417
Johnston, Percy 15
Jones, Lloyd 397
Jong, Erica 286

Index

Jonson, Ben 32, 80, 161, 458

Jordan, Barbara 67

Jordan, David Starr 190, 276

Jordan, Michael 106, 415

Joplin, Janis 368

Joubert, Joseph 111, 119, 157, 236, 326

Jung, Carl 268

Juvenal 459

Kahn, Otto H. 39

Kanin, Garson 128

Kant, Immanuel 212

Karr, Alphonse 68

Kazan, Elia 412

Keats, John 47, 48, 295, 381

Keillor, Garrison 94, 98, 322

Keller, Helen 48, 63, 75, 192, 214, 218, 330, 411, 415

Kelly, Vesta M. 296

Kempis, Thomas à 142

Kennedy, Edward M. . . . 196

Kennedy, Eugene 156

Kennedy, Florynce R. . . .402

Kennedy, John F. 32, 40, 41, 55, 115, 116, 149, 180, 264, 281, 309, 332, 334, 413, 419, 445

Kennedy, Robert F. 414

Kent, Rockwell 31

Keppel, Francis 119

Kerouac, Jack 270

Kettering, Charles F. . . . 60, 172, 416

Keyes, Ken, Jr. 363

Kierkegaard, Soren 149, 277

King,
Martin Luther, Jr. 131, 132, 179, 202, 219, 248, 250, 286, 291

King, Stephen 124

Kingsley, Charles 105, 383

Kipling, Rudyard 340

Klotsche, J. Martin 468

Knox, John 194

Koestler, Arthur 437

Koran 259

Krishnamurti 147

Kuhn, Maggie 21

Kundera, Milian 255

La Follette, Suzanne 150

Lactantius 249

Landers, Ann 316, 438

Landor, Walter Savage 476

Langer, Susanne K. 36

Larkin, Philip 269, 422

Larson, Doug 280
Lauder, Harry 172
Law, William 423
Lawrence, D. H. . . 269, 431
Le Carré, John 378
Leach, Bernard 446
Leach, Reggie 392
Lebowitz, Fran 96, 369
Lec, Stanislaw J. 326
Le Guin, Ursula K. 288
Lehrer, Tom 374
Leigh, Vivien 44, 254
Lennon, John 271,
    358, 445
Leonard, George B. 112
Leopold, Aldo 298, 301
Lerner, Max 239, 338
Lessing, Doris 24
LeSueur, Meridel 458
Levant, Oscar 213
Levenson, Sam 64
Levine, Mel 392
Levi-Strauss, Claude 462
Levy, Judith 89
Lewin, Kurt 192
Lewis, C. S. 449
Lewis, Joe E. 277
Lilienthal, David 177
Lin Yutang 217, 316
Lincoln, Abraham . . . 71, 104,
    109, 132, 141, 233, 318, 337,
    338, 356, 360, 405, 406, 471
Lindbergh,
    Anne Morrow 466
Lindbergh, Charles A. . . . 57
Lindsay, Vachel 268
Lindsey, Ben 22
Lippmann, Walter 287,
    448, 467
Little, Mary Wilson 253
Livy 426
Lobel, Arnold 387
Locke, John 140, 402, 471
Lombardi, Vince 185, 344
London, Jack 428
Longfellow,
    Henry Wadsworth 160,
    191, 203, 284, 324, 372
Loos, Anita 454
Lowell, Amy 42
Lowell, James Russell 175,
    187, 225, 252, 436, 437
Lower, Arthur R. M. . . .469
Loyola, Ignatius 182
Lubbock, John 297
Lucan 304
Lucas, E.V. 224
Luckman, Charles 393
Luther, Martin 333, 334,
    371, 377, 433

Index

Lyly, John 85, 304, 305

Lynd, Robert 464

Lyons, George Ella 313

Mabie, Hamilton 376

MacArthur,
Mary Hardy 367

Macaulay,
Thomas Babington . . .469

MacDonald, George 432, 435, 475

MacDuff, John Ross 186

MacFarlane, Linda 161

MacLeish, Archibald 263

Malcolm X 333

Mandela, Nelson 421

Manikan, Ruby 114

Manley,
Mary de la Rivière . . . 425

Mann, Horace 71

Mann, Stella Terrill . . . 12, 195

Mannes, Marya 352

Mansfield, Katherine 155, 410

Marceau, Marcel 373

March, Fredric 223

Marcos, Imelda 273

Marden, Orison S. 145, 224, 354

Marie, François 156

Markova, Dawna 66

Márquez,
Gabriel Garcia 320

Marquis, Don 389

Marryat, Frederick 372

Marshall, Catherine 197

Martialis,
Marcus Valerius . . 270, 450

Martin, Everett Dean 109

Mary, Queen of Scots . . . 424

Massinger, Philip 473

Maugham, W. Somerset . . . 47, 238, 277

Mauriac, François 293

Maurois, André 34

Maxwell, William 216

McCarthy, Mary 20, 310

McClure, Robert 409

McCormick,
Anne O'Hare 335

McFee, William 91

McGinley, Phillis 319

McGinnis, Pearl Y. 423

McKenney, Ruth 444

Mead, Margaret 21, 62, 257, 318, 396

Menander 25, 127, 198, 274

Mencius 83, 86, 92, 163, 205, 399, 450, 452

Mencken, H. L. . . . 288, 382

Menninger, Karl 287

Meredith, George 254, 290, 298, 374, 412, 441, 443

Michelangelo 33, 39

Michelet, Jules 119

Millay, Edna St.Vincent 46, 90, 381

Miller, Cheryl 341

Miller, Henry 31, 60, 145, 220, 239

Milton, John 326, 351, 366, 473

Mitchell, Donald Grant 124

Mitchell, Laura Lee 348

Mizner, Wilson 141, 251, 452

Molière . . . 162, 288, 324, 404

Monroe, Marilyn 455

Montagu, Mary Wortley 367

Montaigne, Michel E. de . .12, 22, 272, 274, 306, 370, 403, 450

Montapert, Alfred A. . . .146

Montessori, Maria 91

Moodie, Susanna 314

Moody, D. L. 80

Moore, George 246

Moore, Thomas 28, 106, 294

Morell, Thomas 181, 221

Morgan, Charles 462

Morley, Christopher 47, 199, 267, 286, 392, 442

Morley, John 271

Morrison, Herbert 399

Morton, Thomas 347

Moser, Claus 120

Mosley, Oswald 331

Mother Teresa 100, 184, 259, 275, 393, 457

Motherwell, Robert 31

Mountbatten of Burma, Earl 138, 269

Mueller, George 142

Muggeridge, Malcolm 92

Muir, John 301

Murdoch, Iris 101, 286

Murray, Sir James 349

Mussorgsky, Modest 42

Muste, A. J. 333

Naquib 464

Nathan, George Jean 34, 42

Nehru, Jawaharlal 41, 125, 328, 405, 408

Newman, Cardinal 57

Newton, A. Edward 217

Newton, Sir Isaac 95, 233
Nhat Hanh, Thich 68
Nicholson, Jack 47
Nicole, Pierre 378
Niebuhr, Reinhold 59, 228
Nietzsche, Friedrich 206, 245, 446
Nightingale, Earl 392
Nin, Anaïs ... 53, 70, 155, 224
Nixon, Richard 131, 339, 342, 439, 442
Nizer, Louis 16, 346
Noble, Carrie 27
Noble, Vernon 74
Nock, Albert Jay 112
Noonan, Peggy 221
Novalis 82, 228, 401
Nyquist, Ewald B. 135
Ohmae, Kenich 58
Oldenburg, Claes 35
Olsen, Tillie 320
O'Malley, Austin 225, 375
Omartian, Stormie 326
O'Rourke, P. J. 316
Ortega y Gasset, José 422
Orwell, George 132, 352
Osler, William 268
Otis, James 265
Overstreet, Harry A. 26

Ovid 118, 283
Paglia, Camille 170
Paige, Satchel 16, 344
Paine, Thomas 353, 367, 478
Paley, Grace 307
Palmer, Thomas H. 342
Panin, Nikita Ivanovich 195
Parker, Dorothy 456
Parker, John 56
Parker, Theodore ... 367, 433
Parks, Gordon 410
Parks, Rosa 67
Pascal, Blaise ... 232, 250, 295
Pasteur, Louis 341, 349, 350
Patel, Priya 431
Patton, George S. 49
Paul, Jean 18
Paulsen, Gary 313
Peale, Norman Vincent 342, 391, 396
Peguy, Charles 218
Penn, William 293
Pepys, Samuel 233, 259, 456
Perkins, Anthony 317
Perón, Eva 178
Perot, H. Ross 344

Persius 343
Peter, Laurence J. 131
Petit-Senn, John 179
Petrarch 291, 446
Phaedrus 165
Phelps, C. C. 374
Phelps, William Lyon 22
Phillips, Wendell 117, 195
Phillpotts, Eden 324
Phocion 81
Picabia, Francis 262
Picasso, Pablo 35, 41,
    91, 93
Pickett,
    George Edward 327
Pinchot, Gifford 476
Pirsig, Robert M. 68
Plath, Sylvia 253
Plato . . . 14, 82, 122, 164, 427
Plautus, Titus Maccius 81,
    213, 326, 470
Player, Gary 123
Plutarch 201, 343
Poe, Edgar Allan 209, 292
Polanski, Roman 87
Pollock, Channing . . . 55, 211,
    366
Pope, Alexander 83, 116,
    178, 303, 457
Pound, Ezra 110, 176

Powell, Adam Clayton . . . 136,
    151
Powell, William 19
Prevért, Jacques 209
Price, Leontyne 135
Pritchard, Michael 20
Prochnow, Herbert V. . . . 99,
    116, 280, 403
Protagorist 208
Proust, Marcel 237, 240,
    385
Proverb
    African 234
    Dutch 245
    English 54
Quarles, Francis 181, 472
Quiller-Couch,
    Sir Arthur 355
Quinault, Philippe 466
Raban, Jonathan 243
Rabelais, François 256
Rabinwitz, Zadok 223
Rainborowe, Thomas 234
Raleigh, Sir Walter 293,
    432
Rand, Ayn 478
Randolph, John 50
Reade, Charles 45, 56, 81
Reagan, Nancy 285
Reagan, Ronald 56, 150,

152, 225, 240, 420

Reed, Thomas Brackett . . . 65

Reed, Willis 187

Reik, Theodor 123

Reynolds, Joshua 72

Richter, Jean Paul 49, 459

Rickenbacker, Edward 76

Riis, Sharon 384

Rilke, Rainer Maria 289, 364

Robertson, James Oliver . . . 69

Rochefoucauld, François de la 280, 289, 360, 364, 441, 448

Rockefeller, John D. III 321, 459

Rodenbeck, Becky 354

Rodin, Auguste 138

Roe, Anne 150

Roethke, Theodore 306

Rogers, Will 258

Rollin, Charles 232

Ronsard, Pierre de 427

Rooney, Mickey 394

Roosevelt, Eleanor 103, 183, 224, 248, 338, 415

Roosevelt, Franklin D. 36, 70, 93, 133, 144, 149, 152, 219, 253, 265, 335, 336, 341, 359, 366, 400, 442

Roosevelt, Theodore 51, 124, 126, 335, 416, 466

Rosenblatt, Roger 332

Rossetti, Christina Georgina 289

Rossetti, Dante Gabriel . . . 45

Rostand, Jean 19, 435

Roth, Philip 96

Rousseau, Jean-Jacques 107, 281, 369, 379

Rowan, Carl T. 59

Royce, Josiah 331

Rubin, Jerry 17, 370

Rubinstein, Artur 394

Rudikoff, Sonya 345

Rudolph, Wilma 368

Runes, Dagobert 24

Rushdie, Salman 111

Rusk, Dean 376

Ruskin, John 31, 87, 120, 298, 453

Russell, Bertrand . . . 209, 210, 218, 272, 294, 464, 467, 475

Russell, George W. 43

Ruth, George Herman "Babe" 418

Saint-Evremond,

Seigneur de 101

Saint Exupéry,
Antoine de 97, 238,
276, 283

Saint-Simon,
Comte Henri de 171

Salk, Jonas 355

Samuel, Viscount 133

Sand, George 211

Sandburg, Carl 94, 312,
336, 459

Sanger, Margaret 320

Santayana, George 108,
116, 160, 181, 246, 275, 282,
329, 443, 468

Santos, Robert 332

Sapirstein, Milton R. . . 319,
321

Sarason, Irwin 157

Sassoon, Vidal 129

Satre, John-Paul 150

Savile, George Marquess of
Halifax 424

Scalpone, Al 354

Schael, Anne Wilson 424

Schmidt, Benno C., Jr. . . . 154

Schopenhauer, Arthur 25,
93, 106, 449

Schuller, Robert 50

Schulz, Charles M. 212

Schurz, Carl 191, 330

Schwab, Charles M. 72,
212, 216

Schwarzenegger,
Arnold 458

Schwarzkopf, General H.
Norman 82

Schweitzer, Albert . . . 84, 158,
211, 394

Scott, Sir Walter 83, 292,
326, 406, 411

Scott-Maxwell, Florida . . . 316

Seldon, John 158, 474

Seneca, Lucius Annaeus . . . 29,
208, 261, 325, 422, 460, 472

Service, Robert W. 345,
429

Sexton, Anne 320

Seymour, Charles 441

Shadwell, Thomas . . . 291, 461

Shakespeare, William 28,
30, 69, 82, 84, 92, 106, 158,
165, 194, 201, 283, 304, 334,
375, 404, 407, 425, 441, 449,
451

Shakur, Tupac 225

Shallow, Oswald 166

Shaw, George Bernard 27,

Index

60, 137, 227, 322, 436, 447

Shaw, Henry Wheeler 442

Sheehy, Gail 59

Shelley, Mary Wollstonecraft
.... 188, 420

Shelley, Percy Bysshe 125, 284

Shepard, Paul 310

Shepard, Sam 33

Sheridan, Richard Brinsley
.... 75, 364, 379

Sibelius, Jean 104

Sidney, Sir Philip 78

Sigourney, Lydia H. .... .322

Sills, Beverly 31, 414

Simms,
  William Gilmore ..... .100

Singer, Isaac Bashevis 301, 364, 401

Sitwell, Edith 373

Slim, W. J. .... .410

Smiles, Samuel 68

Smith, Florence 27

Smith, Hannah Whitall ... 312

Smith, Lillian 114, 242

Smith, Logan Pearsall 23, 190, 393

Smith, Minnie 366

Smith, Sydney, of Macaulay
.... 207, 430, 470

Smollett, Tobias G. 53

Snow, Carrie 308

Socrates 81, 196, 462, 474

Solomos, Dionysios 266

Solzhenitsyn,
  Aleksandr ...... .413, 444

Sophocles 121, 208, 291, 351, 419, 425, 473

Sosa, Dan, Jr. 395

South, Robert 179, 376

Southey, Robert 374

Spencer, Herbert 57, 119

Spenser, Edmund 63, 84

Spinoza, Benedict ... 229, 333 338, 474

Spring-Rice, Sir Cecil ... 327

Spock, Benjamin 98, 429

Spolin, Viola 137

Spyri, Johanna 335

Stafford, William 297

Stark, Freya 63

Staten, Linda 228

Steele, Sir Richard 364

Stegner, Wallace 300

Stein, Ben 215

Steinbeck, John 101

Steinem, Gloria 321

Stekel, Wilhelm 18

Stendhal 78, 291

Stern, Judith 139

Index

Sterne, Laurence 56, 201

Stevenson, Adlai 171, 269, 307, 328, 332, 336, 356, 364, 468

Stevenson, Robert Louis 163, 217, 240, 241, 346

Stewart, Potter 248

Stilwell, Joseph 102

Stoppard, Tom 309, 442

Storey, David 368

Strauss, Oscar S. 328

Streeter, Edward 244

Streisand, Barbara 393

Stringer, Arthur 174

Studdert-Kennedy, G. A. 402

Sugden, Joe 54, 441

Sun-Tzu 337

Swedenborg, Emanuel . . . 287

Sweet, Ben 369

Swetchine, Anne 157

Swift, Jonathan . . . 14, 26, 36, 65, 245, 276, 477

Swindoll, Luci 156

Switzer, Maurice 231

Syberberg, Hans-Jurgen . . . 37

Syrus, Publilius 187, 237, 378, 423, 427, 458

Szasz, Thomas 88

Tada, Joni Eareckson 201

Taft, Robert A. . . . 126, 265

Tagore, Rabindranath . . . 407, 422, 427

Talbert, Bob 107

Talmud 267

Tanner, Mary Jane Mount 104

Tarkington, Booth 16

Tatara, Walter T. 13

Tawney, R. H. 469

Taylor, Henry 207

Taylor, Mildred D. 146

Teale, Edwin Way 301

Tecumseh 372

Temple, Shirley 395

Temple, William 454

Tennyson, Lord 165, 202, 294, 363, 405, 467

Terence 12, 224, 247, 337,419

Teresa of Avila, Saint 194

Thackeray, William Makepeace . . 56, 159, 204, 257, 322, 475

Thatcher, Margaret 343, 362, 367, 390, 478

Theocritus 159

Theophrastus 427

Thomas, Dave 397

Thomas, Dylan 418

Index

Thomas, Norman 261

Thompson, Dorothy 173, 263

Thompson, Francis 198

Thoreau, Henry David . . . 61, 133, 141, 157, 188, 224, 226, 230, 269, 271, 272, 281, 303, 381, 382, 385, 409, 431, 434, 436, 443, 445, 447, 453, 465, 466, 475

Thucydides 53, 162, 454

Thurber, James 270

Tillich, Paul 77, 146

Tolkien, J. R. R. 309

Tolson, Melvin B. 400

Tolstoy, Leo 37, 38, 60, 124, 196, 207, 323, 439

Toomer, Jean 276

Toscanini, Arturo 384

Tournier, Paul 241

Tremain, Rose 271

Trudeau, Pierre Elliott . . . 351

Trudell, Dennis 311

Trueblood, D. Elton 278

Tubman, Harriet 413

Tucker, Anne 35

Tucker, Sophie 11, 460

Tuckerman,
Henry Theodore 323

Tupper,

Martin Farquhar 373

Turgenev,
Ivan Sergeyevich 371

Turner, Charles 242

Turner, Dale E. 227

Turner, Ted 231

Twain, Mark 16, 55, 89, 102, 105, 118, 148, 170, 231, 258, 270, 329, 330, 366, 368, 371, 377, 389, 412, 444

Tyler, Anne 342

Tzu, Lao 239

Ulmer, Ernestine 275

Updike, John 66, 226

Ustinov, Peter 290

Valéry, Paul 349

van Buren, Abigail 79

van Dyke, Henry . . . 307, 311

van Gogh, Vincent . . . 37, 50, 198

van Halen, Eddie 103

van Loon,
Hendrik Willem 35

Vaneigem, Raoul 165, 296, 440

Vauvenargues 451

Victoria, Queen of England 362, 389

Virgil 27, 292, 365, 431

Voltaire 65, 127, 134,

153, 195, 308, 350, 388, 471

von Hofmannsthal,
Hugo 17

von Leibniz, Gottfried
Wilhelm 284

von Moltke, Helmuth . . . 406

von Schiller, Friedrich 76,
215

von Schiller, Johann 46,
193, 223, 335

von Schlaggenberg,
Kajetan 29

Vreeland, Diana 44

Wadsworth, William 303,
405

Wagner, Richard 211

Wallace, Lew 44

Wallace, William Ross . . . 315

Walsh, James J. 260

Wang, Al 393

Warhol, Andy 169

Warner, Charles Dudley
. . . . 177, 282, 386

Warren, Earl 103

Washington, Booker T.
. . . . 128, 205, 362, 396, 429

Washington, George 153,
159, 338, 438

Washington, Martha 309

Watts, Isaac 83, 165, 477

Wayne, John . . . 169, 377, 447

Webster, Daniel 247, 248,
331

Weil, Simone 235

Welch, Kevin 273

Weller, Peter 241

Wells, Charles 58

Welty, Eudora 241

Wesley, John 455

West, Mae 43, 101, 210,
447

White, E. B. 298

White, Partick 118

White, Stewart E. 100

White, William Allen 204,
264

Whitefield, George 123

Whitehead,
Alfred North . . . 238, 401,
409, 469

Whitman, Harold 477

Whitman, Walt 11, 43,
169, 199, 280, 305, 311

Whittier,
John Greenleaf 406

Whittington, Robert 73

Widdemer, Margaret 88

Wiersbe, Warren 168

Wiggin, Kate Douglas 98

Wigglesworth, Edward . . . 217

Index

Wilbur, Ray L.   90

Wilcox, Ella Wheeler 69

Wilde, Oscar 32, 34, 37, 89, 90, 104, 159, 435, 456

Wilder, Thornton . . . 228, 382, 402

Will, George 90

Willard, Lynn 399

Williams, Robin 321

Williams, Sarah 312

Williams, Tennessee 207, 239, 277

Willkie, Wendell 131, 262, 264

Wilson, A. N.   354

Wilson, Angus 222

Wilson, Harold 71

Wilson, Sloan 48

Wilson, Woodrow 73, 80, 145, 147, 148, 162, 176, 229, 337

Wiman, Erastus 252

Winchell, Walter 100

Winder, Barbara W.   216

Winfrey, Oprah 349

Winner, Charley 396

Winters, Jonathan 399

Winterson, Jeannette 222, 410

Wittgenstein, Ludwig 258

Wolf, Christa 297

Wolff, Tobias 23

Woodberry, George E. . . . 143

Woodcock, George 41

Wooden, John 115

Woollcott, Alexander 274

Wordsworth, William 97, 98, 232, 251, 305, 307, 375, 378, 380

Wright, Frank Lloyd 29, 237, 437

Wright, Richard 153

Wriston, Henry M.   411

Wu Ming Fu 354

Wycliffe, John 435

Wykeham, William of 81

Wylie, Philip 263

Yankwich, Leon R.   319

Yeats, WIlliam Butler 38, 118, 122

Yogananda, Paramahansa 157

York, Peter 46

Young, Dwan 315

Young, Edward 302, 401

Young, Owen D. 49

Zeno 306

Zitkala-Sa 299

Zola, Emile 40

Wendy Toliver would like to extend a special thanks to Lynn Gray, Billie Gray, and Nikki Bleau for their contributions. And to Collin and Miller, her little giant inspirations.

IF YOU LIKED THIS BOOK, YOU'LL LOVE THIS SERIES:

Little Giant® Encyclopedia of Aromatherapy • Little Giant® Encyclopedia of Baseball Quizzes • Little Giant® Encyclopedia of Bizarre Coincidences • Little Giant® Encyclopedia of Card & Magic Tricks • Little Giant® Encyclopedia of Card Games • Little Giant® Encyclopedia of Checker Puzzles • Little Giant® Encyclopedia of Dream Symbols • Little Giant® Encyclopedia of Etiquette • Little Giant® Encyclopedia of Feng Shui • Little Giant® Encyclopedia of Fortune Telling • Little Giant® Encyclopedia of Games for One or Two • Little Giant® Encyclopedia of Handwriting Analysis • Little Giant® Encyclopedia of Home Remedies • Little Giant® Encyclopedia of Inspirational Quotes • Little Giant® Encyclopedia of IQ Tests • Little Giant® Encyclopedia of Leadership Gaffes • Little Giant® Encyclopedia of Logic Puzzles • Little Giant® Encyclopedia of Lucky Numbers • Little Giant® Encyclopedia of Magic • Little Giant® Encyclopedia of Meditations & Blessings • Little Giant® Encyclopedia of Mensa Mind Teasers • Little Giant® Encyclopedia of Names • Little Giant® Encyclopedia of Natural Healing • Little Giant® Encyclopedia of Numerology • Little Giant® Encyclopedia of One-Liners • Little Giant® Encyclopedia of Outrageous Excuses • Little Giant® Encyclopedia of Palmistry • Little Giant® Encyclopedia of Proverbs • Little Giant® Encyclopedia of Puzzles • Little Giant® Encyclopedia of Runes • Little Giant® Encyclopedia of Spells & Magic • Little Giant® Encyclopedia of Superstitions • Little Giant® Encyclopedia of The Zodiac • Little Giant® Encyclopedia of Toasts & Quotes • Little Giant® Encyclopedia of Wedding Etiquette • Little Giant® Encyclopedia of Wedding Toasts • Little Giant® Encyclopedia of Word Puzzles

Available at fine stores everywhere.